CAREER SKILLS LIBRARY

Research and Information Management

THIRD EDITION

CAREER SKILLS LIBRARY

FERGUSON

CAREER SKILLS LIBRARY

Research and Information Management

THIRD EDITION

Ferguson Publishing
An imprint of Infobase Publishing

Research and Information Management, Third Edition

Ferguson
An imprint of Infobase Publishing
132 West 31st Street
New York NY 10001

Library of Congress Cataloging-in-Publication Data

Research and information management. — 3rd ed.
    p. cm. — (Career skills library)
  Includes bibliographical references and index.
  ISBN-13: 978-0-8160-7777-9 (alk. paper)
  ISBN-10: 0-8160-7777-0 (alk. paper)
  1. Information retrieval—Juvenile literature. 2. Research—Methodology—Juvenile literature. 3. Business report writing—Juvenile literature.
I. Ferguson Publishing.
  ZA3080.R47 2009
  025.5'24—dc22
                                2009010619

Ferguson books are available at special discounts when purchased in bulk quantities for businesses, associations, institutions, or sales promotions. Please call our Special Sales Department in New York at (212) 967-8800 or (800) 322-8755.

You can find Ferguson on the World Wide Web at http://www.fergpubco.com

Text design by David Strelecky, adapted by Erik Lindstrom
Cover design by Takeshi Takahashi
First edition by Joe Mackall

Printed in the United States of America

MP ML 10 9 8 7 6 5 4 3 2 1

This book is printed on acid-free paper.

CONTENTS

INTRODUCTION

According to March 2003 data from Nielsen/ NetRatings, over 122 million Americans can sit in their family rooms and email somebody in China or search through the shelves of a university library in England. Many of us have daily access to the wealth of information available online.

It is a very sad thing that nowadays there is so little useless information.

—Oscar Wilde, British poet and playwright

It used to be that having access to information is what separated the educated from the uneducated. Either young people had the money to attend college (where nearly all information used to be), or they didn't. Having access to what we know about the world used to be the key to a young person's success.

Now, nearly everybody can have access to the same information if they have access to a computer and an

Even in the late 1800s, Oscar Wilde commented on the excessive quantity of information available. (Ann Ronan Picture Library/HIP/ The Image Works)

Internet connection. Does this mean we will all be just as prepared for the future? Of course not. More than at any other time in history, we have to know what to do with all the information out there. All information is not created equal. You need to learn how to acquire, evaluate, organize, maintain, and (finally) present information.

All information is not created equal.

Scott begins each busy day as a real estate consultant trying to catch up with what has happened since he last sat at his desk.

"I feel like I'm behind even when I get to work early," Scott said. "I'm going to need to set up a cot next to my desk."

By the time Scott reads through his faxes, email messages, voicemail messages, mail, and any documents and memos that have landed on his desk since he left work the day before, his first hour or two of work is gone, and he still has to act on this new information. He has to answer some of it, file a portion of it, think about a lot of it, and throw some of it away.

A study by the Institute for the Future, the Gallup Organization, Pitney-Bowes, and San Jose University in California discovered what Scott and most people in schools and offices already know: Thanks to all the new technology, most of us are experiencing communication gridlock.

The study was based on responses from more than 1,000 employees of *Fortune* 1,000 companies. It found that workers send and receive an average of 178 messages each day. These messages are sent and received by technology we did not even have until recently: email, voicemail, faxes, text message, and pagers.

The telephone accounted for 24 messages a day, and email and voicemail were responsible for 25 messages. When you think of Scott finally catching up after a few hours on the job, think of this: According to the study, Scott and 84 percent of other workers will be interrupted by new information at least three times every hour.

There's a compelling reason to master information and news. Clearly there will be better job and financial opportunities. Other high stakes will be missed by people if they don't master and connect information.

—Everette Dennis, American author and educator

You already know that information is coming at us at an unprecedented rate. Just turn on your TV or log on to the Internet and you will be reminded of just how much information is out there. Being able to manage this information could be the deciding factor between making it and not making it in today's workforce.

This book is designed to help you handle living in the Information Age. It will show you how skilled you are already at researching and managing information, and it will give you some tips on how to do it better. The book deals with important aspects of research and information management, such as acquiring and evaluating information, interviewing, observation, computer research and storage, library research, and surfing the Internet.

Perhaps, and most important of all, this book will give you a general introduction to the basic technological tools people use to manage information, such as spreadsheets, databases, and word-processing programs.

The book will also introduce you to people like Scott, rookies in the workforce who are doing well in their chosen careers but who had to learn a few things about information management the hard way. Part

HOW MANY PEOPLE ARE ONLINE WORLDWIDE?

Asia/Pacific	578,538,257
Europe	384,633,765
North America	248,241,969
Latin America	139,009,209
Africa	51,065,630
Middle East	41,939,200
Oceania	20,204,331

Source: Internet World Stats, June 2008

of their contribution to this book is to make sure you do not have to learn the same way they did.

This book covers the following:

- How to research using different tools such as observation, interviewing, the Internet, and traditional resources such as books and periodicals

- How to evaluate primary and secondary sources for accuracy, timeliness, and relevancy

- How to organize your information using spreadsheets, databases, and word-processing programs

- How to give insightful presentations and write clear memos

- How to make infographics such as line graphs, bar graphs, and pie charts illustrate your data

- How to keep your information timely and manageable

WELCOME TO THE INFORMATION AGE

Millions of years ago, a creature with hair covering 99 percent of his body woke up, scratched himself, and looked around. He had no idea that he was living in the Pleistocene epoch.

He didn't know in which time he was living for a couple of reasons. First, his brain was much less developed than your brain, and a less developed brain can hold less knowledge. Second, he didn't know he was living in the Pleistocene epoch because historians and scientists had yet to come along and give the period its name.

But we don't need historians or scientists to tell us we are living in the Information Age. All we need to do is look around. There is hardly a house in the United States that doesn't have at least one TV. Some of these televisions have hundreds of channels. Satellite dishes beam in signals from around the world. Emails provide business professionals and the general public with constant updates about any topic

✔ TRUE OR FALSE?

Are You Ready for the Information Age?

1. There are more than 101 million Web sites on the Internet.

2. We acquire, evaluate, and communicate information every day.

3. It's important to know many ways of presenting information.

Test yourself as you read through this chapter. The answers appear on pages 19–20.

imaginable. Facsimile (fax) machines send pages of information from a city in Alaska to a country in Africa in a matter of seconds. More information can be stored on a computer chip the size of a freckle than can be stored in a roomful of file cabinets.

Information is the oxygen of the modern age. It seeps through the walls topped by barbed wire; it wafts across the electrified borders.

—Ronald Reagan, U.S. President

And if this weren't enough, there's the Internet. By definition, the *Internet* is the name for the vast collection of interconnected computer networks around the world. By typing a word into a *search*

Tiny microchips allow for the efficient and convenient storage and retrieval of information that we are accustomed to today. (Christian O. Bruch/Visum/The Image Works)

engine (which allows you to search information on the Internet by subject), millions of pages of information are instantly at your disposal. According to the Hobbes Internet Timeline, there are more than 101 million Web sites currently on the World Wide Web—a number that is growing nearly every month.

DAILY INFORMATION

Although the vast amount of available information can be daunting, you have been acquiring, evaluating, organizing, maintaining, interpreting, and communicating information all of your life. You probably have learned something about the past by listening to your parents tell stories from their childhood. You know your best friend's favorite football team after asking him. You've searched through pages of the newspaper to find exactly which movie is playing at what time at the cinema closest to your house. You know how long it usually takes a wound on your arm to heal.

One aspect of my work that is always changing is the management of information—or, as we sometimes say in the library world—information resources. At the public library, we have books, magazines, newspapers, maps, puppets, Web pages, pamphlets, DVDs, and CDs, just to name a few types of resources. The ways in which we identify, store, loan, and track each of these types of resources varies somewhat based on the material; for example, the cataloging, placement of the item in the library building, and loan period are different for DVDs than they are for paperback books. In addition to managing the information resources themselves, the tools we use to do the managing—computers, software, security strips, etc.—also change. So my work helping to manage information is both varied and key to the library's goal of serving the community.

—Anne Paterson, cataloging librarian, Outagamie Waupaca Library System

In short, you've used and continue to use the basics of information management almost automatically on a daily basis. When you look through the newspaper (either in print or online) to find a movie listing, you are searching a document. You discover your friend's favorite team by using interviewing techniques, and you learn a little something about the healing process by observing the scratch on your arm as it changes from open skin, to scab, to new skin.

Consider the following research scenario involving iguanas. Which of these methods will help you find out about iguanas?

- Talking to the pet-store manager about iguanas
- Reading about them in your encyclopedia
- Looking them up on a CD-ROM or computer database
- Watching what they eat
- Talking to your friend who has one
- Doing a word search on "iguana" on the Internet
- Dangling an iguana in your grandmother's face on Thanksgiving
- Spending an hour watching iguanas at the pet store

- Watching a documentary on the mating habits of iguanas

- Holding and petting an iguana

Although at least nine of the items on the preceding list are solid sources of information, even dangling an iguana in your grandmother's face could tell you something about them. In this case, you could learn how iguanas react when somebody screams. Do they try to scamper away? Do they close their eyes? Do they freeze up? After your grandmother recovers, you might interview her about the experience. She might tell you why the iguana scared her. Maybe her feelings reflect the feelings of other people, which could help explain why more people have dogs and cats as pets rather than iguanas. Researching is easier than you may think.

BOOKS ABOUT TECHNOLOGY

Baig, Edward C. *Macs For Dummies*. 10th ed. Hoboken, N.J.: For Dummies, 2008.

Gookin, Dan. *PCs For Dummies*. 11th ed. Hoboken, N.J.: For Dummies, 2007.

Levine, John R., Margaret Levine Young, and Carol Baroudi. *The Internet For Dummies*. 11th ed. Hoboken, N.J.: For Dummies, 2007.

THE KEYS TO MANAGING INFORMATION

In order to research and manage information effectively, you must be adept at the following practices: acquiring and evaluating information; organizing and maintaining information; and interpreting and communicating information.

Acquiring and Evaluating Information

Although Chapters 2 and 3 spend more time on these concepts, let's take a look at one way we acquire and evaluate information on an ordinary weekend.

Take the movie example we talked about earlier. You have a goal: You want to see a particular movie. You also want to know the showtimes and locations. Immediately, you have decisions to make. You could ask your brother who went to see the movie last week. You could also ask your friends or your parents. You could check the Internet. You could pick up the phone and begin calling local theaters. You could find the movie section in the newspaper and search the listings.

Say you choose the newspaper. You locate the movie listings and find your movie. You're delighted that the movie you're dying to see, *Attack of the Killer Iguanas,* is showing at the only theater within walking distance of your house. You're just about to call a friend when you notice the date on the newspaper. It's a week old. It's possible, maybe likely, that the movie information is out of date. You search the

✍ EXERCISE

What is your favorite method of searching for and retrieving information: the Internet? Books? Periodicals? How often do you use this tool and why do you prefer this research method?

house for this morning's paper and find that the movie is playing at another local theater.

In this ordinary scenario, you have decided what you needed to know, acquired the information, and evaluated the information for relevance and accuracy.

This same process is played out in schools and businesses all over the country. The information may be different and the process may be a bit more complicated, but the basics are the same.

Organizing and Maintaining Information

In simple terms, organizing and maintaining information means keeping track of information in some kind of systematic fashion.

Chris has just finished his second year as a junior stockbroker. He learned a great deal about business and marketing in his part-time jobs during high school and from his courses in college. But there was one important aspect of his job that he'd been practicing since he kept a baseball-card collection in an old shoebox. Throughout most of his years in grade school and even into high school, Chris collected baseball cards. However, his hobby went far beyond collecting the cards of his favorite players.

"I loved keeping track of how a card's worth went up or down," Chris said. "I got a rush out of trying to guess who would be worth what and when. I had a pretty elaborate system worked out as a kid."

Chris printed each player's name in the left-hand column of a piece of paper. He then wrote 10 consecutive dates across the top of the rest of the page and drew lines separating each date. He kept these sheets of paper tacked to the back of his bedroom door and

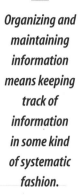

Organizing and maintaining information means keeping track of information in some kind of systematic fashion.

You may not realize it now, but you may be using an organizational tool, such as a spreadsheet, to keep track of your collectible card collections. (Jeff Greenberg, The Image Works)

updated the value of each card periodically. By adding up the totals, Chris could discover at a glance and with a quick calculation what his collection was worth. Without even knowing it, Chris was using a spreadsheet. (Spreadsheets are discussed in detail in Chapter 4.)

"I had trouble keeping a straight face at meetings when my bosses talked to me about computer spreadsheets," Chris said. "I just kept thinking of those yellowed pages tacked to my bedroom door."

☞ FACT

The first computer spreadsheet program was created by Dan Bricklin and Bob Frankston and was called VisiCalc. This program was never patented but heavily influenced modern spreadsheet programs, such as Microsoft Excel.

Source: Dan Bricklin's Web site
(http://www.bricklin.com)

Interpreting and Communicating Information

In his book, *The Call of Stories: Teaching and the Moral Imagination,* psychiatrist and writer Robert Coles recounts his first years as a psychiatrist. He had the devotion and the education. He was ready to take on the world of psychiatry and the people in it. But the more he reported on the mental health of his patients to his superiors, the more one elderly psychiatrist in particular wanted to hear the personal stories of Coles's patients. He didn't want Coles to read medical jargon from a chart; he wanted to hear the stories these patients had to tell. And so Coles began listening to, and telling, stories.

Ironically, Coles had grown up in a home where stories were read and told all the time. His parents had read all the "classics" and often told their son versions of these tales as bedtime stories. But by the time he earned his degree and then joined the workforce, Coles seemed to forget how important narration is to communicating information.

As you'll see later in this book, telling stories is just one way of interpreting and communicating information. It is important to be aware of and schooled in as many ways of presenting information as possible. Depending on your audience, purpose, and goals, you may choose a complex multimedia presentation or a simple oral presentation. You may use overheads, slides, graphics, or audio equipment.

It is important to be aware of and schooled in as many ways of presenting information as possible.

Putting It All Together

There are nearly as many ways to communicate information as there are types of information. In the next example, one ambitious young woman discovers she needs a variety of ways to present information regarding why she is the best person for the job.

Jill was only 21 years old when her father asked her if she'd run his roofing business for a few weeks during the summer while he recovered from a minor operation. Jill was astute enough to anticipate the suspicious looks she'd get from potential customers used to seeing a man climbing out of a roofing truck.

However, Jill had some experience in the roofing business. She had kept her father's books for a couple of years and had even interviewed prospective employees. She needed to decide how best to communicate what she knew to potential customers.

Luckily for Jill and her father, this wasn't the first time she needed to persuade others. As the lead singer and the only female in a rock band in high school, Jill was responsible for scheduling gigs for her group. She played recordings of her band's performances and booked the group's auditions. "But we weren't getting the number of gigs we should have been getting," Jill said. "I knew we were good, but there were a lot of good bands out there. So I decided we needed to sell ourselves, not just our sound."

Soon Jill began taking the rest of the band along with her when she went to speak to other high schools or clubs.

"People saw how we interacted, how we got along, how much fun we had with each other, *and* heard our music," Jill said. "Things went better after that."

So the summer of her father's operation, Jill knew what she had to do. She needed to sell her own image. She took pictures of the houses the company had shingled in the past. She requested and got written references from happy customers.

"I knew I could demonstrate to prospective customers that my father's company was a good one," Jill said. "As they looked at pictures and read customer referrals and recommendations, I talked to them about my role in the company. No numbers or pictures were going to do that for me."

Jill drew on a number of different methods of interpreting and communicating information she learned both as a musician and as a fledgling roofing contractor. She used audio (her band's recordings), graphics (the roofing photographs), written communication (customer referrals), and oral presentations (talking to customers about herself).

As Jill's story shows, we've come a long way since the Pleistocene epoch. Most of us no longer communicate with only grunts and pointing. However, even the most educated and worldly people can become daunted by the sheer amount of information now out there. Many of us find ourselves as bewildered by Web pages and software as Pleistocene creatures would have been by an electric shaver.

However, you already possess many of the information-management skills necessary to succeed in the business world of the next century.

You already possess many of the information-management skills necessary to succeed in the business world.

✔ TRUE OR FALSE: ANSWERS

Are You Ready for the Information Age?

1. There are more than 101 million Web sites on the Internet.

True. In fact, according to the Hobbes Internet Timeline there were 101,435,253 Web sites in November 2006. Learning how to assess the quality and accuracy of information on the Web is an important skill in the Information Age.

2. We acquire, evaluate, and communicate information every day.

True. You may not know it, but you gather information constantly throughout your day—using all five senses: sight, hearing, taste, smell, and touch.

3. It's important to know many ways of presenting information.

True. Knowing how to convey information in writing, orally, by using graphics and video, and through audio is key to success in the workplace.

IN SUMMARY . . .

- Computers not only bring us a wealth of information, but provide many handy ways to organize and present it.

- The Internet has more than 101 million sites full of information and will continue to grow.

- Without even realizing it, you acquire, evaluate, and communicate information every day.

- Newly acquired information should always be evaluated for relevancy and accuracy.

- Using spreadsheets and telling stories are just two ways to organize and communicate information.

- The methods of research and information management can (and should) be combined to create best results.

2

ACQUIRING RESEARCH SKILLS

Most of us have seen countless images of the stereotypical scientist making discoveries. The scientist, usually a man, works in a dark and dank laboratory, surrounded by test tubes and smoking, bubbling beakers. He has a creepy assistant who remains at his side as he labors for hours and hours, never seeing daylight, never living life outside of the laboratory.

But if this were the only way to acquire information, very little information would ever be acquired. Not too many people want to spend their days trapped in the dark with a creepy assistant. Information is everywhere, and there are a variety of ways to get to it.

Some of the most effective ways of obtaining information include observation, interviewing, traditional resources, and actual experience. Before we talk about the latest and most pervasive—the Internet—we'll

✔ TRUE OR FALSE?

Do You Have Good Research Skills?

1. When conducting interviews it's a good idea to avoid asking questions that will elicit "yes" or "no" responses.

2. An encyclopedia from 1999 should be my primary source of information when conducting research for a report on the history of sports in China.

3. All information on the Internet has the same value.

Test yourself as you read through this chapter. The answers appear on pages 41–43.

take a look at the more traditional ways of acquiring information.

OBSERVATION

Young adults are often chastised for hanging out. But hanging out can be a great way of acquiring information.

From 1960 to 1962, the writer Gay Talese hung out. He wanted to write a book on the building of the Verrazano-Narrows Bridge, which was being built to connect Staten Island to Brooklyn, New York.

Gay Talese spent many hours in observation to write his book The Bridge, *proving that even just "hanging out" is a way of gathering information about a place and its inhabitants.* (Peter Kramer, Associated Press)

According to Barbara Lounsberry, the author of the article "Portrait of an (Nonfiction) Artist," Talese "practiced the fine art of hanging out" while working on his book, which became *The Bridge*. For two years, Talese hung out near the bridge, watching the workers walking the beams and eating their lunches hundreds of feet in the air.

"I was so regularly in attendance at the bridge in my off-hours and vacations from the *New York Times*

Even if you're hanging out at the local mall, you could be acquiring information.

that I was practically considered one of the staff of U.S. Steel," Talese said.

Even if you're hanging out at the local mall, you could be acquiring information, depending on how much attention you're paying to your surroundings. For instance, just by visiting the mall on a Monday and on a Friday, you could begin to acquire information. Do more people shop on Fridays or Mondays? Are shoppers alone on Monday and with somebody else on Friday? Do more women shop on Monday than on Friday? Do men shop alone?

Now, of course, you couldn't draw too many conclusions or make grand generalizations from just hanging out at the mall for two nights. (Remember,

✏ EXERCISE

- Name one place where you enjoy the act of observation. What are you looking at? Why do you enjoy it? What conclusions can you make about the location, people, wildlife, etc.?

- Pick a room in your house and spend five minutes studying its contents (chairs, table, books, artwork, etc.) Go into another room and write down everything that you remember seeing. Compare you list with the room's actual contents to determine the strength of your observational skills.

Talese hung out for two years to write *The Bridge*.) But it could be a start to learning more about the shopping habits of mall mavens, if that were indeed your goal.

Hanging out could also lead to another way of acquiring knowledge, and that's through interviews.

INTERVIEWING

Let's say you've come to the conclusion that more women seem to shop alone on Monday nights than on Friday nights. You've been observing this phenomenon at the mall for two weeks and now you want to check the accuracy of your hunch. What do you do?

While Talese hung out at the bridge, he got to know many of the workers. They learned what he was doing, talked to him almost every day, and began to trust him. Soon he was able to begin interviewing. Because you probably won't have two years to spend on most of your information-gathering projects, you'll have to shorten the process.

If you've been hanging out at the mall for any length of time, you've probably seen some of the same faces night after night. Let's say the manager of the shoe store has smiled at you a time or two. Maybe you've even exchanged greetings. She could be a good person to interview. You could ask her if she has some time to be interviewed at her convenience. Begin the interview by telling her your name and the purpose of the interview—whether it's for a school project or for your own curiosity. Here's how Andy handled just such an assignment.

For as long as he could remember, Andy had dreamed of becoming a photographer. He had taken pictures at every family wedding and each family vacation since he was old enough to hold a camera.

"At my cousin's wedding, I didn't take any pictures of the bride," Andy said. "I was too interested in the people wandering to and from the bar."

Andy's first job out of college was not his dream job. Instead of having his own studio and being his own boss, Andy had to earn money by working with a studio photographer who specialized in baby pictures. His first assignment was to find out which day of the week at a local mall was the most popular shopping day among women with babies. His boss had rented space for a temporary studio in a nearby mall for a special one-day promotion, and he wanted to make sure there would be plenty of traffic from moms with babies and toddlers.

"I really didn't know what to do," Andy said. "I didn't think there would be some kind of book on it, so I went to the mall, did some people-watching, and talked to some store clerks. By the time I was out of there, I felt pretty confident."

Andy was lucky. Not only was he naturally observant, having a photographer's eye, but he was charming and polite. He interviewed the assistant manager of a sporting goods store who had worked in the mall for almost 10 years. Soon the sporting goods manager took Andy to several other mall employees, including some who worked at stores specializing in children's clothing. Andy asked them when mothers with babies were most likely to shop. Almost everyone he spoke to said that their shops were packed on Monday and Tuesday mornings with moms with small children. Andy reported this information to his boss, who scheduled his display for Monday morning and took more than 100 baby pictures on the day of the event.

"At the time I didn't think much about it," Andy said. "But when I quit my job and set up my own business as a wedding photographer, the first thing I did was interview recently married couples about what they liked and disliked about their wedding photos. I really knew the value of interviewing and how I could be more successful."

Interviewing is a great way of finding out what other people know, and people are almost always a researcher's greatest resource. And yet the more we observe about the people and the "things" in our environment, the more likely we are to see almost everything as a potential source of information. Tina, a licensed practical nurse in a nursing home, learned this lesson by sitting in a comfortable chair in her great-grandmother's house.

Though she had been to her great-grandmother's house many times, she looked around the dining room and noticed things she didn't remember seeing

The more we observe about the people and the "things" in our environment, the more likely we are to see almost everything as a potential source of information.

before. A framed poster hung on the wall above her great-grandmother's oak hutch. In it, a young man appears to be drowning. Behind him a ship sinks into a storm-racked ocean. Beneath him is a caption reading, "Loose lips sink ships."

INTERVIEWING TIPS

- Ask permission first, and state your purpose honestly.

- Establish a prearranged time and place. Stick to the time limits you state.

- Putting yourself at ease is the best way to put an interviewee at ease. Use role-playing or conduct practice interviews first.

- Come prepared with a list of questions that you need answered.

- Begin with "safe" questions. Ask general questions about the interviewee's job or expertise, the spelling of his or her name, etc.

- Be patient. Give the interviewee time to respond. Let the interviewee fill the silence.

- Take careful notes. If you use a tape recorder, be sure to obtain permission from the interviewee first.

- Don't be judgmental. Don't ask questions just to confirm what you already believe.

Tina recognized the caption as something Americans at home were told during World War II as a warning not to divulge information that might be useful to the enemy.

- Try to avoid questions that elicit a "yes" or "no" answer unless it's a survey questionnaire. Open-ended questions encourage more conversation.

- Don't stare, but don't avoid eye contact either.

- Be aware of body language and cultural and gender differences regarding body language.

- Do not be afraid to ask the interviewee to repeat a response if you think you might have misunderstood what he or she said.

- Do not be afraid to ask questions that arise during the interview.

- Leave open the possibility for a second interview. For example, ask, "If I have any more questions, is it okay if I call you?"

- When you are at home or work typing your interview notes, do not hesitate to call the interviewee to double-check quotes or facts. The person probably will not mind being called again. He or she will mind being misquoted, however.

"As I looked at the poster, I couldn't help wondering whether some of my patients had fought in World War II. What did they go through?" Tina said. "I used to think I had nothing to learn from my patients. Now, I view them differently. I started asking some of them about what they remembered most about World War II. Some of them really opened up and told me some fascinating stories. Talking about their experiences really lifted their spirits and it kept me inspired to work for them. I think I'm a better nurse now."

☞ FACT

Empiricism is a 17th-century British theory stating that all knowledge is derived from sensory experience, by observation, and experimentation.

TRADITIONAL RESOURCES

Generally, the best place to begin any research project is in the library. Although there is a glut of information available, a library search using reference works can be the best way of seeing the whole and the parts. For example, if you're interested in the Roman Empire, an encyclopedia will present an overview and will also break down the discussion of the Roman Empire into sections on economics, government, labor, etc., which could be the first step in narrowing the focus of your research.

The best place to begin any research project is in the library.

✍ EXERCISE

Interview a family member about his or her childhood. Ask approximately 10 questions; then write a short report about what you learned. This will test your interviewing, note-taking, and listening skills. Ask your interviewee to read your report. Ask your interviewee if your report accurately represents what was said and how he or she likes how you present the information.

Reference works include encyclopedias, dictionaries, bibliographies, indexes, atlases, handbooks, and almanacs. In no way should your research be confined to these sources. However, they are often a good place to begin. Scanning these sources can help you focus the angle for your research. Also, reference works will lead you to more specific and detailed sources.

Periodicals, including newspapers, magazines, and journals, are also important resources. Magazines are publications for the general public. They often cover a variety of issues and appeal to a wide range of readers. The advantage of magazines is their timeliness—especially now that many are available on the Internet. Most magazines come out weekly or monthly, allowing them to keep up with current trends and events better than books can, while still

Equipped with a large supply of books, periodicals, and electronic resources, the library is a good place to research information. (Jeff Greenberg, The Image Works)

being able to offer more in-depth coverage than newspapers.

Journals differ from magazines in one fundamental way: Journals are usually designed and published for a very specialized audience. For instance, the *Journal of American Folklore* has a much smaller and more specialized readership than *People* magazine. This distinction does not make one a more valuable research tool than the other, just different.

But before you begin paging through past issues of hundreds of magazines and newspapers to locate an article on your subject, consult indexes such as the *Readers' Guide to Periodical Literature* or use online tools such as LexisNexis (a fee-based service) to help you locate specific issues and topics.

Books, of course, will be listed in the library's catalog alphabetically by the author's last name, but you can also search by subject and title.

Many of the indexes and other research texts can also be found on CD-ROMs, in Portable Document Format, and online. Many libraries subscribe to commercial information services that provide reports and the like from publishers and other corporations. These types of services usually charge a fee.

Another excellent source of information is the Educational Resources Information Center (ERIC). ERIC contains indexes, abstracts, and, in some cases, publishes the full text of nearly 1,000 education journals. ERIC publications can be found online at http://www.eric.ed.gov.

Knowledge is of two kinds. We know a subject ourselves, or we know we can find information about it.

—Samuel Johnson, English author

EVALUATING TRADITIONAL SOURCES

You can begin to determine a source's usefulness and relevance to your needs by first scanning the introduction, table of contents, indexes, and headings. Also, try to answer these questions about the sources you choose:

- Does the source devote attention to your topic?
- Is the source specialized enough to meet your needs?
- Does it treat topics in too detailed or too superficial a way?
- How current is the source?
- What are the author's credentials?
- What is the author's bias?
- What do other experts say about this book or about its author?

THE INTERNET AND THE WORLD WIDE WEB

There's no doubt that careful observation, purposeful interviewing, and traditional resources can get you a long way in the information game. But we live in a time when we have access to an electronic, global library. At one time, people had to travel to

✍ EXERCISE

Think about the last time you conducted research for a school assignment. What traditional resources, if any, did you use? What are your preferred tools for research?

Alexandria, Egypt, where the first—and for a time the only—library in the world was located. Now we need only venture into our homes, schools, or offices.

The ability to conduct thorough and accurate research is a necessary skill in the advertising business. Working with clients typically involves coming up with several ideas for different campaigns for the client's products, whether that's shampoo, credit cards, or cereal. And it's extremely important that we've researched a number of topics, including the client's product, what types of campaigns the client has already used, how others with the same type of product advertise, and what's been effective before presenting the campaign ideas. It's also critical to keep in mind that the research should have a global perspective (What's been working well in Japan?) and the research should look at a variety of formats (Is the Web site working well? What about a digital billboard?). In addition to looking "outside" to research, it's important to look within our organization and go through our archives. After all, it would be pretty silly to pitch an idea that hasn't worked well in the past or that the client didn't even like. Many people in advertising—on the account side, the creative side, the planners—need to do research as part of their jobs. And some people, such as those in the corporate information center, do research as their primary responsibility.

—Jan Clayton, advertising copy editor

As stated earlier, the *Internet* is the name for the vast collection of interconnected computer networks around the world, which enables users to:

- Access newspapers, electronic books, and journals

- Search library catalogues from around the world

- Search a wide variety of databases

- Seek information from experts

- Send and receive email

The *World Wide Web*—the "www" in Web addresses, or URLs—resides on the Internet. Just as the Internet is a system of interconnected computer networks, the Web refers to the interconnected information.

EVALUATING INTERNET RESOURCES

Web sites and the documents featured on them need to be evaluated for usefulness and relevance just like traditional resources. Here are a few questions to ask about Web sites and materials you find on the Internet:

- Who is the author? What are his or her qualifications?

- Does the Web site or author provide citations that reference where the information was obtained?

- Who is the sponsor of the Web site?

- When was the Web site or document last updated? Does the information seem current? Do Web links still work?

- Does the Web site or document seem objective or biased? What is the target audience?

- Does the information cover what you need? Or is too simple or too complicated?

CONDUCTING A WEB SEARCH

Let's say Tina wanted to find out more about the loose lips and sinking ships of World War II. Here are the initial steps she most likely would have to take:

1. She'd begin by activating her Web browser, such as Windows Internet Explorer, Mozilla Firefox, Safari, or Opera.

2. She'd pick a search engine, such as Yahoo! or Google, and direct her browser to go to the site.

3. When Tina saw a search box, she'd type in her keywords and click "search."

4. Or instead of manually searching her subject, she could choose a topic area from within the directory. For example, if she used Yahoo!, she could select the education area from the Yahoo! menu, which would lead her to history and eventually to World War II. She'll still have a great deal of information to sort through before getting to information on loose lips and sinking ships.

Remember, anybody can put something on the Web. This means that even somebody's Aunt Martha who believes she not only fought as a submarine captain in World War II but lived during the Pleistocene epoch could show up on your Internet search. This

POPULAR WEB BROWSERS

Internet Explorer
http://www.microsoft.com/windows/
downloads/ie/getitnow.mspx

Mozilla Firefox
http://www.mozilla.com/en-US/firefox

Safari
http://www.apple.com/safari

Opera
http://www.opera.com

AOL Explorer
http://downloads.channel.aol.com/
browser

Avant Browser
http://www.avantbrowser.com

Google Chrome
http://www.google.com/chrome

K-Meleon
http://kmeleon.sourceforge.net

is the reason that being able to evaluate information (the subject of Chapter 3) is critical.

The ultimate search engine would basically understand everything in the world, and it would always give you the right thing. And we're a long, long ways from that.

—Larry Page, founder of Google

✔ TRUE OR FALSE: ANSWERS

Do You Have Good Research Skills?

1. When conducting interviews it's a good idea to avoid asking questions that will elicit "yes" or "no" responses.

True. Open-ended questions will encourage interviewees to provide more detailed responses, which are important if you want to gather a large amount of useful information.

2. An encyclopedia from 1999 should be my primary source of information when conducting research for a report on the history of sports in China.

False. Always use the most current resources. If you used an encyclopedia with a 1999 copyright date for your research report on China, you would have missed learning that China hosted the Olympics in Beijing in 2008 and that in 2002, Yao Ming, one of its star basketball players, began a successful career in

MAJOR INTERNET WEB PORTALS AND SEARCH ENGINES

AltaVista
  http://www.altavista.com

Excite
  http://www.excite.com

Go.com
  http://go.com

Google
  http://www.google.com

Lycos
  http://www.lycos.com

Yahoo!
  http://www.yahoo.com

the National Basketball Association—raising the profile of Chinese sports throughout the world. Today, most encyclopedias—and many other research resources—are available online, so it is best to use these resources rather than dated materials.

3. All information on the Internet has the same value.

False. If you needed information about the pros and cons of coronary artery bypass surgery,

FIVE QUESTIONS FOR INFORMATION HUNTERS

1. Where should I begin (e.g., observation, interview, Internet)?

2. Do I know exactly what I'm looking for? You may find great information that is of no use to you at a particular time.

3. How much time do I have? Sometimes, you can get the right answer in a big hurry by picking up the telephone and calling your local university, library, or a local expert.

4. How will I know when I'm through researching?

5. What will I do with the information once I have it?

would you consider information from the American Medical Association's Web site and the Web site of an individual who had this type of surgery in 2001 to have equal value? The answer is obviously no. Be sure to seek out reliable sources when you use the Internet for research.

IN SUMMARY . . .

- Observation, interviewing, traditional and online resources, and experience are all useful ways to obtain information.

✍ **EXERCISE**

Choose a topic you are discussing in one of your school classes or that could help you on your part-time job. Next, spend some time acquiring as much information as you can on that subject by using observation, interviewing, and the Internet. Which method were you most comfortable with? Which helped you the most? Which helped you the least? Why?

- Observation can be as simple as just "hanging out."

- Interviewing is a good tool for research because people are researchers' greatest resources.

- Traditional resources (encyclopedias, magazines, newspapers, books) are great sources for information but need to be first evaluated for accuracy, timeliness, and relevance.

- The Internet has revolutionized the way people conduct research, but surfers beware: Be sure the information you read is backed up by reliable sources!

3

EVALUATING INFORMATION

Never before has so much information been at our fingertips. And everybody, or nearly everybody, has access to the same information you do. This makes being able to look at information critically and to evaluate it carefully the skill that could distinguish you from the countless people who have access to the Internet and 200 channels on their televisions.

Information's pretty thin stuff unless mixed with experience.

—Clarence Day, American author

THE IMPORTANCE OF EVALUATING INFORMATION

Almost every job today requires information-evaluation skills. What information is relevant? What

✔ TRUE OR FALSE?

Do You Know How to Evaluate Information?

1. Even reputable sources sometimes have their own agendas.

2. When faced with information overload on the Internet, it's important to remember your original research goal.

3. Information from government and private agencies is often overlooked by researchers.

Test yourself as you read through this chapter. The answers appear on page 62.

information should you believe? What information is out of date? Doctors, lawyers, and business managers have to carefully sift through and evaluate information on a daily basis. But the importance of such skills is perhaps most easily seen in a career such as journalism.

Megan, a reporter for a midsize daily newspaper for over a year, was becoming a little restless for "the big story." One morning, Megan received a phone call from a woman who said she had information about how a local hospital was mistreating its elderly patients. Although the woman wouldn't give Megan her name, she did agree to meet her at a restaurant near the newspaper.

SURF THE WEB: EVALUATING INTERNET RESOURCES

Evaluating Information Sources: Basic Principles
   http://library.duke.edu/services/instruction/
   libraryguide/evaluating.html

Evaluating Internet Sources and Sites: A Tutorial
   http://www.lib.purdue.edu/ugrl/staff/sharkey/
   interneteval

Evaluating Web Pages
   http://library.duke.edu/services/instruction/
   libraryguide/evalwebpages.html

Evaluating Web Sites: Criteria and Tools
   http://www.library.cornell.edu/olinuris/ref/
   research/webeval.html

Five Criteria for Evaluating Web Pages
   http://www.nmc.edu/library/how/internet/five.
   html

The Good, the Bad, and the Ugly or, Why It's a Good
Idea to Evaluate Web Sources
   http://lib.nmsu.edu/instruction/evalcrit.html

How Do I Evaluate Internet Resources?
   http://www.bc.edu/libraries/help/howdoi/howto/
   evaluateinternet.html

The woman appeared credible. She told story after story about elderly patients being abused by orderlies, nurses, and doctors. When Megan asked for the names of the patients, the woman told her that they were all afraid to talk to a reporter. All communicating would have to be done through her. Because of the importance of the story and because Megan could understand the trepidation of elderly people who had already been victimized, she agreed to the woman's conditions.

Megan then arranged interviews with the hospital's media-relations spokesperson and several nurses. She was told by everybody that an orderly had been fired five years ago for neglecting patients, but that there had been no other incidents at the hospital before or after.

Doubting the hospital's version of its patient care, Megan gained permission to interview current patients. Although some people complained about the food or about having to buzz the nurses several times, Megan recognized these were minor complaints.

She then checked the public record for any reports filed against the hospital but found nothing particularly horrifying. After several discussions with her editor and her source, Megan dropped the story.

"I've never been more embarrassed in my life," she said. "It's like I had blinders on. Every other source seemed to contradict what this woman was telling me, but I shut everything else out."

DOT WHAT?

When conducting research on the Web, it's important to know what types of Web sites you are visiting. Web suffixes, or domains— such as ".com" or ".org"—will provide you with a clue to the site's founder, and to the quality and type of information that the site provides. Here are some examples:

.com	for-profit companies
.edu	educational institutions
.org	nonprofit organizations
.gov	government agencies
.int	international organizations
.mil	U.S. Department of Defense
.info	unrestricted usage
.biz	business organizations

Megan placed the woman's information above every other piece of information out there and learned the hard way that all information is not created equal.

We all evaluate information every day. If somebody you don't trust or who is always telling rumors tells you something, you're probably not going to believe the person. What Megan didn't know and didn't take the time or effort to find out was that the woman who made the allegations had recently been fired from her cleaning job at the hospital. She refused to give her name because Megan would have discovered that her informant had an ax to grind. And as many reporters know, information coming from a grinding ax is usually exaggerated or just untrue.

Have you ever been in a situation similar to Megan's predicament? Perhaps you heard some misleading gossip about a schoolmate and took it to be the truth. Such situations are valuable lessons about the importance of evaluating information.

The more gross the fraud, the more glibly will it go down, and the more greedily be swallowed, since folly will always find faith where imposters will find impudence.

—Charles Caleb Colton, British author

Information coming from a grinding ax is usually exaggerated or just untrue.

PRIMARY SOURCES

Whenever possible, you should rely on primary sources for your information. But as Megan discovered, even primary sources—in this case her own interviews—can be suspect and should be held to intense and thoughtful scrutiny.

Primary sources are firsthand, generally contemporaneous accounts, including letters, speeches, historical documents, eyewitness reports, works of literature, firsthand reports on experiments and surveys, and, of course, your own observations, interviews, and correspondence. In a court of law, a letter written the day after an event occurs is almost always regarded as more telling evidence than, say, six months later. The same is true when it comes to historical evidence. A dispatch written by a general from the battlefield has greater credibility than what he says in his memoirs written 20 years later. Why? Because not only do memories fade over time, but 20/20 hindsight leads us to reshape our recollections to fit what happened later or to put our own thoughts and actions in a better light.

When you have acquired all firsthand, primary information, it will be up to you to evaluate and draw your own conclusions.

SECONDARY SOURCES

The next best origins of information are secondary. *Secondary sources* are reports or analyses of information drawn from other (often primary) sources. Examples of secondary sources include one doctor's evaluation of other doctors' studies, an English professor's reading of a poem, a historian's account of a battle, an encyclopedia, and any of the other reference works discussed in Chapter 2. Secondary sources are useful as a way of summarizing events, so that you as a

TYPES OF PRIMARY AND SECONDARY SOURCES

Primary Sources

- Autobiographies
- Constitutions, statutes, presidential proclamations
- Diaries
- Firsthand accounts
- Historical documents
- Interviews
- Letters
- Meeting minutes
- Memoirs
- One's own observations, interviews, and correspondence
- Oral histories
- Original research in an academic journal
- Personal journals
- Photographs
- Some government documents
- Some newspaper articles
- Speeches
- Videos
- Wills
- Works of literature

Secondary Sources

- Biographies
- Dictionaries
- Editorials
- Encyclopedia articles
- General histories
- Literary criticism
- Popular magazines
- Scholarly literature reviews
- Some government documents
- Textbooks

Source: Valencia Community College Library, The Research Process: A Step-by-Step Guide

SURF THE WEB: USING PRIMARY AND SECONDARY SOURCES

Library Research Using Primary Sources
http://www.aurora.edu/library/
primarysources.htm

Primary Resources
http://www.lib.berkeley.edu/instruct/
guides/primarysources.html

Primary vs. Secondary Sources
http://valenciacc.edu/library/west/
research/sbs_primarySecondary.asp

The Research Process: A Step-by-Step Guide
http://valenciacc.edu/library/west/
research/sbs_primarySecondary.asp

Using Primary Sources on the Web
http://www.ala.org/ala/mgrps/divs/
rusa/resources/usingprimarysources/
index.cfm

Using Sources Effectively in Your Own Writing
http://www.mals.duke.edu/Using_
Sources.pdf

researcher can get a handle on a particular angle or focus.

EUPHEMISMS

Similar to Megan's problem with primary sources, you will need to make an informed judgment about the information from secondary sources. Effective information management means being able to identify false information or facts that might be cloaked in euphemisms, or what the writer George Orwell called the "politics of the English language."

For instance, if a government official releases a statement saying that there was "collateral damage" during a military operation, you need to be critical and realize that this means that there were civilian casualties.

The mainstream press swallowed whole the following now-famous statement that President Ronald Reagan made. Regarding the Iran-Contra scandal, Reagan used the passive voice effectively when he said of the scandal, "mistakes were made." This statement is vague and could be misleading, but it was what the administration wanted the public to think. Amazingly enough, in 1997, President Bill Clinton repeated the exact phrase when asked about campaign fund-raising scandals. As a researcher, you must be aware that even reputable sources have their own agendas to which you must be alert.

✍ EXERCISE

Answer the following questions with a "yes" or "no." To learn about a company you are considering to work for, which of the following would you do?

1. Talk to someone who has worked there for several years

2. Talk to someone who has worked there for a week

3. Check on the company with the Better Business Bureau

4. Look up articles on the company in local newspapers in your library

5. Talk to customers

6. Talk to somebody whom the company fired for stealing

If you answered yes to questions 1, 3, 4, and 5 you are on the right track. These sources will most likely provide you with useful information. Talking to someone who has worked at the company for a week (question 2) won't really give you much information, since the person has very little experience with the company. Talking to someone who has been fired for stealing (question 6) would be the worst choice of this group, since he or she might have an axe to grind with company management. You would also have to question the character of anybody who steals.

Hear one side and you will be in the dark. Hear both and all will be clear.

—Thomas Haliburton, Canadian writer

INFORMATION OVERLOAD

Information overload—having too much information to evaluate—can easily paralyze our ability to make decisions. In most situations, it's simply impossible to pull together all the information available on a subject. We need to focus on the essential information.

With so much information now online, it is exceptionally easy to simply dive in and drown.

—Alfred Glossbrenner, American author

Just after graduating from college, Brendan accepted a job with the National Park Service. His dream was to work with fledgling wolf populations. Whenever he talked with his friends about wolves, they all seemed interested, but nobody else was considering making a living working with wolves.

He set out to learn all he could about the reintroduction of wolves into parts of the western United States. During his first year of employment with the Park Service, Brendan had received positive evaluations from his superiors and made some national connections. Now he had to learn about the wolves of the Rocky Mountain region.

Drawing on his experiences from high school and college, Brendan knew enough to begin his search with periodicals in the library. He read all he could about recent reintroductions of wolves from Canada. He wrote down every name mentioned in the article and every source quoted. He was on his way.

And then he got in trouble.

"All of a sudden I felt overwhelmed," Brendan said. "I thought finding out about wolf reintroduction would be easy. I mean it was a one-time thing, and it just happened. Pretty soon it felt like I had to know everything about everything."

Brendan was faced with an ordinary yet daunting dilemma: How much information was enough? How much was too much?

Brendan soon learned that to talk intelligently about the wolves of the Rocky Mountain region, he needed to find out not only what had happened recently, but what had happened approximately 70 years ago, when thousands of wolves were systematically eliminated from the Rocky Mountain region of the United States. Brendan also decided he should research ranching practices in the region because ranchers were the most vocal opponents of the wolf reintroduction.

Brendan used the Internet to read about wolf reintroduction in parts of Canada and about wolf populations in other parts of the world, including Italy,

Russia, and Israel. At that point, Brendan began to feel overwhelmed by all he didn't know and all there was to know about wolves around the world.

Then it clicked. His goal was to learn enough about the reintroduction of wolves to Yellowstone National Park. He didn't have to become the world's greatest expert on wolves.

He made files for wolf populations around the world and stored that information for future use. Brendan threw out studies on the specific ways that wolf mythology paralleled beliefs held by some modern practitioners of witchcraft. Not that he wasn't interested in wolf mythology, but he understood the value of remaining focused when feasting at the information buffet. Brendan focused on finding out the specifics of the most recent Yellowstone reintroduction, including the reaction of the local ranchers.

The most important thing you can do to avoid crumbling under the weight of information is to know what you're looking for.

Everybody gets so much information all day long that they lose their common sense.

—Gertrude Stein, American author

The most important thing you can do to avoid crumbling under the weight of information is to know what you're looking for. Brendan forgot what the focus of his search was, so he was vulnerable to all information. While your stamina will inform you when it is time to stop interviewing, young adults usually run into trouble with information overload when it comes to library research.

There's a curious thing about information overload: When people feel there's just too much information and they cannot seem to get a handle on all of it, they end up with no useful information at all.

To avoid information overload, keep the following considerations in mind the next time you are researching:

- Know your research task thoroughly.

- Keep a working bibliography and/or take notes.

- Get an overview of your subject first. This means beginning with the reference sources as a way of finding your focus. Check encyclopedias, subject headings in books, and bibliographies.

- Find sources. Check books, periodicals, newspapers, government reports, and statistical sources. When you are deciding which books to use, check the index first. If the book donates only a page or two to your topic, it's probably not the right book for you.

- Choose and read sources with a critical eye to look for relevance and for bias.

- When conducting a Web search, select your keywords carefully. Make sure your keywords are as precise and as accurate as possible. This will help ensure that your search results produce a manageable list of sites. When a search engine produces results in 395,000 sources relevant to your topic, you had better come up with more precise keywords before initiating a new search strategy.

EVALUATE YOUR RESEARCH OPTIONS

When you think you have done all your research and still feel that there might be something you have missed, don't panic. First, take a deep breath, and then check these often overlooked sources:

- Vertical files: pamphlets and brochures from governmental and private agencies

- Special collections: manuscripts and rare books

- Audio collections: records, MP3s, music, readings, speeches, and CD-ROMs

- Video collections: slides, filmstrips, videocassettes, and DVDs

- Art collections: drawings, photographs, and paintings

SHOULD YOU USE WIKIPEDIA TO CONDUCT RESEARCH?

Wikipedia is a free-content encyclopedia written by volunteers from around the world. It is billed as the

✍ EXERCISE

Let's say you have to write a short paper on the Civil War. Define a specific goal for your research (such as Abraham Lincoln's Emancipation Proclamation, which ended legal slavery). Now ask yourself all the places your search might lead you. Which information will you use? Which might you store for the future? Which will you be better off throwing away?

"people's encyclopedia" because anyone (regardless of their qualifications) can write and edit content. This means that some information at the popular site may be completely accurate, while other articles may be partially or even completely inaccurate or biased. Many students use Wikipedia to conduct research, but should you? The answer is no if you adhere to the guidelines for evaluating information detailed in this book. When conducting research, your goal is to find unquestionably accurate information. By using Wikipedia (especially if you do not check it against other sources), you are taking a chance that the information may be incorrect. And learning that your facts are wrong is not what you want to hear after you've turned in a research paper or given a presentation to your coworkers.

Although Wikipedia has implemented changes in the way it edits and reviews its articles to improve their accuracy, it is a good idea to think carefully before relying on it as a source of completely trustworthy information.

✔ TRUE OR FALSE: ANSWERS

Do You Know How to Evaluate Information?

1. Even reputable sources sometimes have their own agendas.

True. When researching a topic on the Web, be sure to find at least three sources to ensure that there is no bias or hidden agenda in the way the information is presented.

2. When faced with information overload on the Internet, it's important to remember your original research goal.

True. It's common to find dozens or even hundreds of links about a topic when you perform a keyword search. The key is to stick to your original goal and only focus on the pages that seem like they will provide answers to your research questions.

3. Information from government and private agencies is often overlooked by researchers.

True. Government and private agencies provide a wealth of free or inexpensive information in print and at their Web sites.

IN SUMMARY . . .

- With the Internet and other advanced researching techniques, sources of information are seemingly limitless. Because of this, the need to evaluate information for credibility is more important than ever.

- Always double-check facts and back up references when getting information from both primary and secondary sources.

- Primary sources, or firsthand experiences and accounts, are reliable but still deserve scrutiny.

- Secondary sources, or information drawn from other sources, should be evaluated more closely than primary sources and supported by several accounts.

- The careful researcher should be alert to euphemisms (commentary that hides or disguises the truth).

- To avoid information overload, always keep your original research goal in mind.

- Research doesn't have to be limited to books; information can be deducted from audio and video collections, rare books and manuscripts, and even pieces of art.

4

NOW WHAT DO I DO WITH IT?

Although so far we have treated the different facets of information management separately (for example, observing, interviewing, evaluating, and organizing), it's likely that when you're in the workforce full time, you'll be performing all of these tasks nearly simultaneously.

In many instances, employees have to organize text (both on paper and on computer) and numbers (usually in the form of graphs, tables, spreadsheets, or databases).

ORGANIZING INFORMATION

Some philosophers have speculated that human beings have a natural urge to organize their environments. Perhaps it's a way of convincing ourselves that we can control the universe in a small way if we have our underwear and socks separate from our swimsuits and our T-shirts and in a different drawer from our jeans. Maybe it's a way to stave off chaos.

✔ TRUE OR FALSE?

Do You Know How to Organize Information?

1. A computer hard drive is very similar to a file cabinet.

2. Using a database is an excellent way to reorganize a card index, dictionary, Rolodex, or phone book.

3. Spreadsheets and databases are excellent ways to electronically store and manipulate information.

4. It's okay to use someone's work without crediting them.

Test yourself as you read through this chapter. The answers appear on pages 89–90.

Human beings have a natural urge to organize their environments.

Even the Pleistocene man in Chapter 1 must have had a way of organizing the spoils of his daily hunt. Surely he separated the meat from the skin and the bones from the teeth. Maybe his subconscious—which he, of course, did not even know he had—let him feel a sense of control over the chaos, or maybe it just made sense to put what he planned to eat in one corner of the cave and what he planned to make tools out of in a different corner.

Again, just as you have been acquiring information most of your life, you've also been organizing information, which probably began by keeping your Transformers separate from your Hot Wheels collection.

DID YOU KNOW?

Employers surveyed in 2007 by OfficeTeam rated organization skills as the most important soft skill in demand among administrative staff at their companies. The ability to write for business and analytical skills ranked sixth and seventh, respectively.

Source: Fitting In, Standing Out and Building Remarkable Work Teams

But anyone can organize information into piles. Where it can get tricky is organizing information that you're still in the process of gathering.

Deleasa works as an assistant in a job-placement firm. Her boss started the company with the sole purpose of matching top-level executives and management personnel with high-tech firms. However, the company soon decided it had better diversify.

Soon Deleasa found herself inundated with resumes from blue-collar and service-technician job seekers as well as executives. "Everybody in the firm was already overworked," Deleasa said. "I knew I had to do something myself and do it quickly or I'd be buried beneath tons of paper. I call it the landfill effect."

☛ FACT

A database is nothing more than an assortment of related information organized in some way.

Deleasa already had a solid database set up for people seeking executive and managerial jobs. She continued to input information for these clients into the existing database. However, Deleasa needed to create an additional database for people seeking service and technical jobs. In the meantime, she had to organize the new flood of paper arriving on her desk into files until the new database was created.

Deleasa quickly got her hands on as many file folders as she could, and she labeled them simply according to jobs the company sought to fill. For example, she had a folder for electricians and another file for people looking for jobs in computer repair. In time, separate subcategories emerged. All the folders containing electricians who also had college degrees went together, separate from those without degrees.

✍ EXERCISE

Were there other ways Deleasa could have organized her information? How would you have done it? Was there a downside to what Deleasa did?

READ MORE ABOUT IT: OFFICE ORGANIZATION

Aslett, Don. *The Office Clutter Cure*. 2d ed. Cincinnati, Ohio: Marsh Creek Press, 2008.

Davenport, Liz. *Order from Chaos: A Six-Step Plan for Organizing Yourself, Your Office, and Your Life*. New York: Three Rivers Press, 2001.

Hansen, Dhawn, and Tracey Turner. *Organize Your Office and Manage Your Time: A Be Smart Girls Guide*. Bloomington, Ind.: iUniverse Inc., 2007.

Kendall-Tackett, Kathleen. *The Well-Ordered Office: How to Create an Efficient and Serene Workspace*. Oakland, Calif.: New Harbinger Publications, 2005.

Nakone, Lanna, and Arlene Taylor. *Organizing for Your Brain Type: Finding Your Own Solution to Managing Time, Paper, and Stuff*. New York: St. Martin's Griffin, 2005.

Nelson, Mike. *Clutter Proof Your Business: Turn Your Mess into Success*. Franklin Lakes, N.J.: Career Press, 2002.

Rockmore, Alicia, and Sarah Welch. *Everything (almost) in Its Place: Control Chaos, Conquer Clutter, and Get Organized the Buttoned Up Way*. New York: St. Martin's Griffin, 2008.

Before she knew it, Deleasa was not only keeping up with her daily entries into the existing computer database, she was organizing the "paper" database by simply slipping an incoming resume into the proper folder. She then asked her boss if she could work overtime on Saturday in order to transfer her paper files to a computer database.

"I panicked for a little while," Deleasa said. "And then I just relied on what I had at my disposal: common sense and a stack of file folders. If I'd tried to create a database and input everything as it came in, it would have been a mess. I wouldn't have known how to structure it and might have had to redo it two or three times."

Organization most often begins by putting like items with like items. The first thing you need to do when organizing any information is determine the major categories. Make sure the categories are inclusive, that all your material will fit into one of your selected categories. For example, from as early as your grade-school years, you probably had one folder for your science class and another for your English class. That was organizing information by categories.

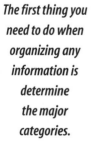

The first thing you need to do when organizing any information is determine the major categories.

The next step is to divide the material you need to organize into the separate, inclusive categories you have chosen. Then see if you need subcategories. Make ongoing adjustments to your organizational strategy when necessary. For example, if you need to add a category, add one. If you need to divide one inclusive category into two, do so.

For years the staple of the office environment has been the filing cabinet. Documents are stored in filing folders, usually alphabetically. Often, one drawer of the filing cabinet contains invoices while another holds work orders. As companies have expanded and evolved, files were stored by date, and then alphabetically by invoices, work orders, etc.

If you look at just about anything, you will notice the layers of organization, like putting your English essays on one side of the folder and your English exams on the other. Even with the advent of new computer storage technology, the same fundamental organizational principles apply: organization within organization.

For example, everyone who uses a computer soon learns that you have to organize the information on your hard drive into logical "directories" and

---

SURF THE WEB:
ALL ABOUT SPREADSHEETS

About.com: Spreadsheets
http://spreadsheets.about.com/od/?once=true&

Answers.com: Spreadsheet
http://www.answers.com/topic/spreadsheet

The Spreadsheet Page for Excel Users and Developers
http://spreadsheetpage.com

"subdirectories." Otherwise, you soon won't be able to find and retrieve anything you've saved on your hard drive. A computer's hard drive is very similar to an old-fashioned file cabinet with drawers (directories) containing file folders (subdirectories) in which you file paper (electronic files).

☛ FACT

It is estimated that 80 percent of the documents we file are never accessed again, according to the *Leader-Post*.

SPREADSHEETS

In Chapter 1 you read about Chris the stockbroker. Chris sat in a meeting with a smile on his face when his managers spoke to him and other employees about the benefits and uses of spreadsheets. Chris had unknowingly used basic spreadsheets to track the value of his baseball-card collection.

Spreadsheet programs can manipulate data almost instantaneously.

A *spreadsheet* is a grid of "cells" formed by rows and columns. Each cell can contain a number or a mathematical formula, and the contents of any cell can be added to, subtracted from, divided by, or multiplied by the contents of any other cell in the spreadsheet. Best of all, anytime you change the contents of one cell, all the other cells linked to it will change accordingly. This function makes repetitive, difficult, and complex calculations (that could take hours to perform using a calculator) a snap. Indeed, spreadsheet programs can manipulate data almost instantaneously, and if you've set up and tested the spreadsheet correctly, these programs can do calculations without ever making a mistake.

For example, let's say you need to begin budgeting your money. You know you have monthly expenses and a fixed income. Here is where a spreadsheet comes in handy. Down the left-hand-side column, list your projected expenses: car, insurance, clothes, entertainment, etc. Along the top row, list the months of the year. Then at a glance you'll be able to calculate how much money you'll need on hand in any particular month.

So far, your spreadsheet looks like Spreadsheet 1.

Spreadsheet 1							
	A	B	C	D	E	F	G
		Jan.	Feb.	Mar.	Apr.	May	Jun.
1	Take-home pay						
2	Savings						
3	Car						
4	Insurance						
5	Clothes						
6	Total essential expenses						
7	Net (take home minus expenses)						

Computer spreadsheet programs, such as Lotus 1-2-3 and Microsoft Excel, do all kinds of sophisticated calculations for you. By changing one number, the program makes any necessary calculations. This is what enables spreadsheets to work out "what-if" scenarios.

Let's say your monthly take-home pay is $700. You need to save $150 a month for college tuition, your monthly car payment is $135, you have quarterly insurance payments of $200, and you typically spend $50 a month on new clothes. These you regard as your essential expenses (note that we put savings first). The money left over after these expenses you can use on less important costs, such as gas and entertainment. If you plug these numbers into the first month of your spreadsheet, it will look like Spreadsheet 2.

Spreadsheet 2							
	A	B	C	D	E	F	G
		Jan.	Feb.	Mar.	Apr.	May	Jun.
1	Take-home pay	$700					
2	Savings	$150					
3	Car	$135					
4	Insurance	$200					
5	Clothes	$50					
6	Total essential expenses						
7	Net (take home minus expenses)						

The spreadsheet program will let you copy numbers across rows. So now you copy across the numbers in rows 1, 2, 3, and 5 because they should be the same every month. You don't copy the $200 for car insurance across because you pay that only once every three months, so you put $200 in cell E4. Now you want to add up your essential expenses for each month by putting a simple formula in cell B6 that looks like this: SUM@(B2..B5). This tells the computer to add up all four cells in column B between rows 2 and 5 and to put the number in B6. If you copy the same formula across row 7, the program "knows" that you want to apply the same formula to each column. The program will calculate the formula SUM@(C2..C5) and place the result in cell C6, calculate the formula SUM@(D2..D5), and place the result in cell D6, etc. Now your spreadsheet looks like Spreadsheet 3.

Spreadsheet 3							
	A	**B**	**C**	**D**	**E**	**F**	**G**
		Jan.	Feb.	Mar.	Apr.	May	Jun.
1	Take-home pay	$700	$700	$700	$700	$700	$700
2	Savings	$150	$150	$150	$150	$150	$150
3	Car	$135	$135	$135	$135	$135	$135
4	Insurance	$200	$0	$0	$200	$0	$0
5	Clothes	$50	$50	$50	$50	$50	$50
6	Total essential expenses	$535	$335	$335	$535	$335	$335
7	Net (take home minus expenses)						

It's time to put in a formula that will tell you what you have available for "discretionary spending," otherwise known as entertainment costs to many people. To do so, put a formula (B1 - B6) in cell B7. This tells the computer to subtract your total essential expenses from your take-home pay so you see what you can afford on entertainment each month. Your spreadsheet now looks like Spreadsheet 4.

It looks as though you have a tighter budget in January and April when you have to make those insurance payments. As a result, perhaps you decide to hold down your entertainment and fuel expenses to $300 in the other four months and save the extra $65 to help you make those quarterly car payments, allowing you to spend an even amount

Spreadsheet 4							
	A	B	C	D	E	F	G
		Jan.	Feb.	Mar.	Apr.	May	Jun.
1	Take-home pay	$700	$700	$700	$700	$700	$700
2	Savings	$150	$150	$150	$150	$150	$150
3	Car	$135	$135	$135	$135	$135	$135
4	Insurance	$200	$0	$0	$200	$0	$0
5	Clothes	$50	$50	$50	$50	$50	$50
6	Total essential expenses	$535	$335	$335	$535	$335	$335
7	Net (take home minus expenses)	$165	$365	$365	$165	$365	$365

on fuel and entertainment (approximately $298) every month.

Now suppose your boss gets generous in March and gives you a salary increase that raises your take-home pay by $50 a month. With this spreadsheet, you simply need to change your take-home-pay line, and the program will (with the use of those formulas) recalculate the other cells accordingly. Your spreadsheet now looks like Spreadsheet 5.

DATABASES

A *database* is an organized collection of information. Databases really prove their worth when you want to take something like a card index, Rolodex,

Spreadsheet 5							
	A	B	C	D	E	F	G
		Jan.	Feb.	Mar.	Apr.	May	Jun.
1	Take-home pay	$700	$700	$750	$750	$750	$750
2	Savings	$150	$150	$150	$150	$150	$150
3	Car	$135	$135	$135	$135	$135	$135
4	Insurance	$200	$0	$0	$200	$0	$0
5	Clothes	$50	$50	$50	$50	$50	$50
6	Total essential expenses	$535	$335	$335	$535	$335	$335
7	Net (take home minus expenses)	$165	$365	$415	$215	$415	$415

✍ **EXERCISE**

Make a list of five things you now do with a calculator that you could do better with a spreadsheet.

---

dictionary, or phone book and completely reorganize it. Let's say you have 50 people in your address book. A computer database would allow you—in a matter of seconds—to further organize your friends and business associates by ZIP code or street address. If you were planning a wedding or a reunion, a computer database would allow you to find out immediately how many people in your address book, for instance, live in your state, how many live in your ZIP code, how many have kids, or any other category of information you have recorded.

THINGS YOU CAN DO WITH A SPREADSHEET

- Financial planning

- Analyzing statistics

- Invoices and bills

- Budgeting

Information is stored in a database using fields and records. In a computer database, each entry from your address book is called a *record*. Just as a page in your book has spaces for names, addresses, and phone numbers, each record in your database has spaces called *fields* (address field, phone number field, etc.). In most database programs, you can fill an almost unlimited number of records and assign as many fields as you need. Each field will have different content, just as each page in your address book has different information.

WORD PROCESSING AND DOCUMENT MANAGEMENT

In the past two decades, the typewriter has been replaced by the desktop computer in practically every office. Word-processing software drove the typewriter into extinction because word-processing software can do everything a typewriter can do, but better. Besides basic typing functions, word-processing programs can:

- Check for and correct misspellings

- Merge a list of names, addresses, and key information with the text of a letter and personalize every letter (called "mail merging")

- Cut and paste blocks of text within one document or from one document to another

Word-processing software can do everything a typewriter can do, but better.

- Find and replace one word or phrase with another word or phrase
- Instantly change the format of a document and the size of the type to fit the page
- Generate tables of contents and indexes automatically
- Insert pictures and graphs into a document
- Format text into columns
- Use a variety of different typefaces and sizes in the same document

These capabilities alone would probably have sealed the typewriter's doom, but word-processing programs enable us to do something even more important. Because they store documents in digital form, they enable us to *manage* documents. We can save them, retrieve them, modify them, copy them, or transmit them around the world without ever leaving our desks.

What does this mean to you? If you haven't already learned the basics of using a word-processing program, do so as soon as you can. Word processing has become so crucial in the business world that you'll need at least basic word-processing skills in almost any office job. Don't think that word processing is just for secretaries. Increasingly, companies are expecting managers and professional workers to type and organize their own documents—so much so, in fact, that the traditional secretary/typist might soon be as extinct as the typewriter. Don't worry too much

WHEN TO USE SPREADSHEETS, DATABASES, OR WORD-PROCESSING SOFTWARE

	Spreadsheets	Databases	Word-Processing Programs
Budget expenses	X		
Track addresses		X	
Track bank accounts	X		
Cutting and pasting text from one document to another			X
Tracking credit card charges	X		
Tracking phone numbers		X	
Financial planning	X		
Keeping inventory		X	
Writing a term paper			X
Setting up a library card catalog		X	
Tracking bills or invoices	X		
Saving letters electronically			X
Tracking value of baseball cards, stamps, rare records, and other antiques	X		
Using a set of form letters			X
Recording and organizing the contact information for potential customers		X	

about what program you learn. If you learn Microsoft Word, you'll be able to pick up Corel WordPerfect or one of the other popular programs very quickly.

Word-processing programs make writing simpler. Whether you are working on a term paper or a letter to a friend, word-processing programs can make your writing legible, neat, organized, and even more correct (with the help of spell- and grammar-checking tools). However, there are some things to keep in mind as you type away.

Plagiarism

Any time you use another writer's words or even a close paraphrase of his or her words, you must give that writer credit. If you don't, you've committed the crime of plagiarism. Simply put, *plagiarism* is using somebody else's words and claiming or pretending that the words are your own. A simple rule of thumb for avoiding plagiarism is: When in doubt, give the original writer credit.

Any time you use another writer's words or even a close paraphrase of his or her words, you must give that writer credit.

It is a poor wit who lives by borrowing the words, decisions, miens, inventions, and actions of others.

—Johann Kaspar Lavater, Swiss theologian and poet

If you're applying common information, you do not have to worry about plagiarism. If you say the Earth is round, nobody will accuse you of plagiarism. On the other hand, if you write a research paper stating that 16.5 percent of all merchant marines get seasick, chances are some poor researcher spent months of his or her life to determine that fact. In this case, the researcher deserves the credit.

LEARN MORE ABOUT IT: PLAGIARISM

Web sites

Avoiding Plagiarism
http://owl.english.purdue.edu/owl/resource/589/01

Center for Academic Integrity
http://www.academicintegrity.org

Plagiarism Lessons
http://www.mtlsd.org/highschool/
highschoolplagiarismlessons.asp

PlagiarismToday
http://www.plagiarismtoday.com

Plagiarism: What It is and How to Recognize and Avoid It
http://www.indiana.edu/~wts/pamphlets/
plagiarism.shtml

Students' Guide to Preventing and Avoiding Plagiarism
http://www.liunet.edu/cwis/cwp/library/exhibits/
plagstudent.htm

(continues)

(continued)

Books

Anderson, Chalon E., Amy T. Carrell, and Jimmyl Widdifield. *What Every Student Should Know About Citing Sources with APA Documentation.* Boston: Allyn & Bacon, 2006.

Lipson, Charles. *Doing Honest Work in College: How to Prepare Citations, Avoid Plagiarism, and Achieve Real Academic Success.* Chicago: University of Chicago Press, 2004.

Posner, Richard A. *The Little Book of Plagiarism.* New York: Pantheon Books, 2007.

Stern, Linda. *What Every Student Should Know About Avoiding Plagiarism.* New York: Longman Publishing Group, 2006.

DID YOU KNOW?

Thirty-six percent of high school students surveyed in 2008 by the Josephson Institute of Ethics said that they "used the Internet to plagiarize an assignment."

✍ EXERCISE

Say you were going to use each of the following in a school paper. Which could raise questions about plagiarism?

1. To be or not to be, that is the question.

2. The Earth revolves around the sun.

3. In Australia, 33 percent of all aboriginal tribesmen accumulate six ounces of earwax every five months.

4. Two paragraphs of information downloaded from a Web page

5. Chapter 3 of this book

If your answer is everything except statement 2, you are correct. Since the second statement is a commonly known fact, it is safe from any charge of plagiarism. The first statement is a quote from Shakespeare and should be attributed to him even though most people recognize it as a line from *Hamlet*. The third statement is obviously such specific information that the researcher who uncovered this (graphic) fact deserves credit. The fourth example also should be credited. Just because something is found on the Internet doesn't mean you should "borrow" it without giving credit where it's due. Finally, the last example is brazen plagiarism.

PLAGIARISM CHECKLIST

1. What types of sources have you used? Your own independent research? Common knowledge? Someone else's material? You must acknowledge it if it is somebody else's material.

2. If you are quoting somebody else's work, is the quotation exact? Have you demonstrated omissions with ellipses or brackets?

3. When paraphrasing or summarizing, have you used your own sentence structure and words? Have you correctly represented the author's words?

4. Are all uses of somebody else's material acknowledged in your text?

5. Does your bibliography or works-cited page include all the sources you have drawn on in your work?

Copyright

Copyright law is far too complex to summarize here, but its basic principle is fairly simple. If you quote some other writer's work extensively and the writer's work is under copyright protection, you must get permission first if you are creating a work of your

WHAT IS COPYRIGHT?

According to the U.S. Copyright Office, copyright is "a form of protection grounded in the U.S. Constitution and granted by law for original works of authorship fixed in a tangible medium of expression. Copyright covers both published and unpublished works. Copyright, a form of intellectual property law, protects original works of authorship including literary, dramatic, musical, and artistic works, such as poetry, novels, movies, songs, computer software, and architecture. Copyright does not protect facts, ideas, systems, or methods of operation, although it may protect the way these things are expressed."

Source: U.S. Copyright Office

own that will be sold for money, such as a book, magazine article, or TV script. What does the word "extensively" mean in this context? It depends on what percentage of the original text you quote, what percentage it will be of the work you are creating, and your purpose in using the other writer's material. Does that mean that if you quote some writer's book in a memo you're writing to your boss, you need to get permission? No. But if you are using an entire chapter of a book in your company's employee handbook, you probably should ask for permission. For more information on copyright, visit the

Web site of the U.S. Copyright Office at http://www.
copyright.com.

PAPER FILES AND COMPUTER STORAGE

As you probably already have observed, more schools
and businesses are becoming increasingly depen-
dent on computer storage. The practice of storing
boxes and boxes of dusty documents is gradually
coming to an end. Why? Office space is expensive.
Corporate executives are realizing that because of
technology—particularly the computer chip—one
employee working at home can do just as much (if
not more) in his or her own home than at the office.
Companies can comprise several people working in
their own homes, sending email and memos and
faxing invoices and price sheets. Even if they all
work in the same building, how can they all have
access to the same data? In other words, where can
all the files be stored so that everyone has quick
access to them in a way that doesn't take up a lot of
physical space?

*Storing and
retrieving
information in
an electronic form
will keep getting
cheaper and more
convenient.*

The answer is computer storage. More and more
businesses seek a paperless office. Some are turning
to more computer storage. Still others are storing
information on CD-ROM, client servers, and external
hard drives.

If there's one prediction that's a safe bet, it's that
storing and retrieving information in an electronic
form will keep getting cheaper and more convenient.

In most offices, paper files may never be completely eliminated, but their importance will diminish compared to electronic records.

✔ TRUE OR FALSE: ANSWERS

Do You Know How to Organize Information?

1. A computer hard drive is very similar to a file cabinet.

True. It has directories (like a drawer in a filing cabinet) that contain subdirectories (file folders) in which you store electronic files (paper files).

✍ EXERCISE

If you currently hold (or have ever held) a part-time office job, do you see opportunities at your office to limit the use of paper files and storage? Is there information that could be stored on computers? Do a quick study and write a memo that could be presented to your boss. Be sure to include cost savings (paper, employee hours, etc.). Also be sure to mention any disadvantages of computer storage. For instance, how would you guard against losing company files if a computer or computer network became infected or crashed?

2. Using a database is an excellent way to reorganize a card index, dictionary, Rolodex, or phone book.

True. Using a database allows you to quickly organize and reorganize information—which will save you time in the workplace.

3. Spreadsheets and databases are excellent ways to electronically store and manipulate information.

Partially true. But don't forget word-processing programs, which allow you to edit, manage, and present large amounts of information.

4. It's okay to use someone's work without crediting them.

False. You should always give credit if you use another writer's words. If you are unsure if you need to give credit, err on the side of caution and give the original writer credit.

IN SUMMARY . . .

- Once you have obtained your information, organize it for easy understanding and future retrieval.

- A spreadsheet is useful for quantitative data because it can be easily manipulated using timesaving keystrokes and formulas.

- Databases are useful for information that can be easily categorized, such as contact information into lines (categories) for names, street addresses, and phone numbers.

- Word-processing programs are not only easier to use than typewriters; they can do much more, including checking for spelling and grammar errors and organizing documents into electronic files.

- Plagiarism can be blatant or subtle, but should always be avoided. All materials used as sources need to be cited.

- The computer chip has made information storage and retrieval faster and more accurate than using paper and file folders.

CREATING EFFECTIVE PRESENTATIONS AND MEMOS

Effective presentations are attention-getting, meaningful, memorable, activating, and balanced. Furthermore, a business presentation is most effective when it satisfies the purpose of presenting, which is to persuade.

—Lani Arredondo, author of *The McGraw-Hill 36-Hour Course: Business Presentations*

Remember Brendan, the National Park Service ranger, who ran into trouble in his search for information when he lost sight of his goal? Like a boat cut loose from its moorings, Brendan found himself adrift, carried in whatever direction the tides happened to be going. Something similar can happen even after you've evaluated and interpreted

✔ **TRUE OR FALSE?**

Do You Know How to Effectively Communicate Information?

1. It's important to fit every last bit of information into a 10-minute presentation.

2. A good presentation has two main components: the body and the conclusion.

3. Memos should contain long, dense paragraphs to provide as much information to the reader as possible.

Test yourself as you read through this chapter. The answers appear on pages 107–108.

information. It's easy to get lost in a sea of information when it comes time to present to others the data you have acquired, evaluated, and interpreted.

ORAL PRESENTATIONS

Let's say you have spent a month acquiring information about a topic that your boss wants you to share with senior management in a five-minute presentation. You know so much that you can't imagine how you're going to fit it all into a short presentation. The first thing to plant firmly in your mind is that you are not going to fit all you know into that five-minute presentation. Senior management won't want to hear all the details, and trying to cram in everything will just confuse your listeners by distracting them from the "big picture."

Remember, the information you leave out of your presentation is not going anywhere. You'll have it if anyone asks for it. Besides, you will look good if you answer more specific questions about your topic after your presentation.

Let's return to Andy (from Chapter 2) for a minute. If you recall, Andy had to hang out at the mall to find out when mothers with babies shopped. Assuming Andy's boss was a busy photographer, he probably would not have a couple of hours to listen to Andy tell him all he learned at the mall. As a matter of fact, let's say Andy's boss happens to be between shoots.

Trying to cram everything in will just confuse your listeners by distracting them from the "big picture."

When giving a presentation, speakers must have focus and direction to keep the attention of their audience and satisfy the needs of their client, boss, or team. (Rogelio Solis, Associated Press)

It's Andy's first big assignment, and he has three minutes to present his information to his boss.

Andy's boss will not want to hear about:

- The price of the new U2 album
- The fact that the young woman behind the jewelry counter smiled at Andy
- That senior citizens walk around the mall's perimeter for exercise
- The hours when women with babies do not shop at the mall

It is not that all of this information is inherently less valuable. If Andy's boss wanted to sell pictures of senior citizens, the fact that they could be found at the mall at certain times would be of utmost importance. But he doesn't. The photographer wants to know when mothers with babies shop at the mall. The goal will determine the focus of the presentation.

The first thing Andy should do is summarize the information he has acquired. He'll be able to do this if he first remembers what the point of the exercise was.

NARROWING THE SCOPE

Andy must first narrow the scope of his material. He cannot possibly tell his boss everything he saw, heard, and learned at the mall. If he loses focus and begins talking about the popcorn that got stuck in

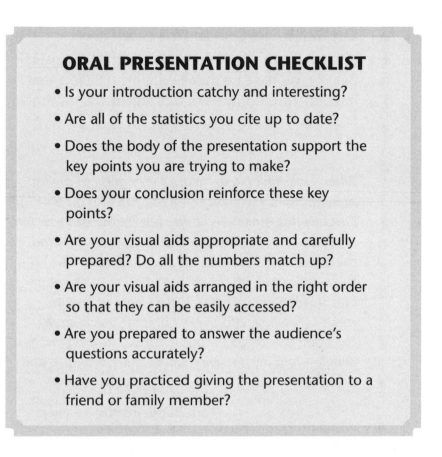

ORAL PRESENTATION CHECKLIST

• Is your introduction catchy and interesting?

• Are all of the statistics you cite up to date?

• Does the body of the presentation support the key points you are trying to make?

• Does your conclusion reinforce these key points?

• Are your visual aids appropriate and carefully prepared? Do all the numbers match up?

• Are your visual aids arranged in the right order so that they can be easily accessed?

• Are you prepared to answer the audience's questions accurately?

• Have you practiced giving the presentation to a friend or family member?

his teeth on his second afternoon at the mall, his three minutes will be over and his boss will know nothing except that perhaps he needs somebody a little more professional than Andy.

In order to narrow his scope, Andy must pick the two, three, or four most important points his boss needs to know in order to decide when to set up shop in the mall.

ORGANIZING THE MATERIAL

The next thing Andy must do is organize his material. He will have no time to ramble. The fact that he has only three minutes makes organizing his presentation even more important.

When I was first hired, I wasn't very good at giving presentations. I would conduct research to prepare, but I usually just threw everything but the kitchen sink into my presentations. This just ended up overwhelming the audience. I soon realized that I needed to be more judicious with the stats and other information I included in my speeches. Once I learned how to conduct research effectively, I became much more confident standing in front of 10, 20, even hundreds of people—and my audience stayed more attentive and asked better questions after the presentation.

—Tom Zane, insurance executive

A good presentation, regardless of its length, has three major components: the introduction, body, and conclusion.

Introduction

The introduction should generally accomplish four basic things:

1. Grab the audience's attention.

2. State the basic topic of the presentation.

3. Connect the topic to the audience.

4. Preview the main points of the body.

Body

The body is usually the meat of your presentation. It includes detail and supporting material. Depending, of course, on the length of the body, it should be divided into three or four sections or main points.

- *Main point #1.* This is your first area of information and is probably your most important point. It should be explained and supported by details.

- *Main point #2.* This is your second area of information and should also be supported by details.

- *Main point #3.* This is your third area of information and should be supported in ways similar to points 1 and 2.

This looks simple and for a very good reason: It is. The difficult part is determining the main points of your presentation and describing them clearly.

Conclusion

The conclusion should accomplish two things:

1. It should review the main points of your presentation.

2. It should provide closure and an ending.

TEN THINGS TO AVOID IN A PRESENTATION

1. Reading from a paper instead of performing a presentation (Instead, speak from a "keyword" outline on note cards. You should be familiar enough with the material to do this.)

2. Talking at or over your audience (People dislike lectures.)

3. Avoiding eye contact

4. Ignoring raised hands or interruptions (Try to see the unexpected as an opportunity.)

5. Being unprepared

6. Saying anything that is considered to be in poor taste

7. Discriminatory language

8. "Apologetic" language (Nobody likes a whiner.)

9. Too many abbreviations or acronyms

10. Overusing "I" in your speech

✍ EXERCISE

Assume you are Andy and you have three minutes to present the information you acquired at the mall. Using information you invent, and remembering your goal (to find out when mothers with babies are most likely to shop), write an introduction. Fill in the three main points of the body and provide a conclusion.

LEARN MORE ABOUT IT: MAKING PRESENTATIONS

Web sites

Effective Presentations
http://www.research.ucla.edu/era/present

How to Deliver Effective Presentations
http://www.ehow.com/how_2265462_deliver-effective-presentations.html?ref=fuel&utm_source=yahoo&utm_medium=ssp&utm_campaign=yssp_art

Humor in Public Speaking
http://www.msstate.edu/org/toastmasters/resources/humor_in_speaking.pdf

(continues)

(continued)

Making Effective Oral Presentations
  http://web.cba.neu.edu/~ewertheim/skills/oral.
    htm

Presentations.com
  http://www.presentations.com

Top 10 Tips for Creating Successful Business
Presentations
  http://presentationsoft.about.com/od/
    powerpointinbusiness/tp/bus_pres_tips.htm

WannaLearn.com: Personal Enrichment: Public
Speaking
  http://www.wannalearn.com/Personal_
    Enrichment/Public_Speaking

Books

Bell, Arthur H. *Butterflies Be Gone: An 8-Step Approach
to Sweat-Proof Public Speaking*. New York: McGraw-Hill,
2008.

PROFESSIONAL MEMO WRITING

Regardless of the communication medium you use, you need to structure and manage the contents of your presentation into a beginning, a middle, and an end. Let's say we try to apply what we learned

Benjamin, Susan J. *Speak With Success: A Student's Step-by-Step Guide to Fearless Public Speaking.* Tucson, Ariz.: Good Year Books, 2007.

Kushner, Malcolm. *Public Speaking for Dummies.* 2d ed. Hoboken, N.J.: For Dummies, 2004.

Macinnis, J. Lyman. *The Elements of Great Public Speaking: How to Be Calm, Confident, and Compelling.* Berkeley, Calif.: Ten Speed Press, 2006.

Maxey, Cyndi, and Kevin E. O'Connor. *Speak Up!: A Woman's Guide to Presenting Like a Pro.* New York: St. Martin's Griffin, 2008.

Weissman, Jerry. *Presenting to Win: The Art of Telling Your Story.* Upper Saddle River, N.J.: Prentice Hall, 2006.

Zelazny, Gene. *Say It with Presentations.* Rev. ed. 2d ed. New York: McGraw-Hill, 2006.

Zeoli, Richard. *The 7 Principles of Public Speaking: Proven Methods from a PR Professional.* New York: Skyhorse Publishing, 2008.

about oral presentations to what has become the most ordinary means of communication: the phone call. Even the ordinary phone call has an introduction: "Hello." What follows the agreed-upon introduction is the body of the phone call. The body,

LEARN MORE ABOUT IT: WRITING AND WORDS

Bell, Arthur H. *Writing Effective Letters, Memos, and E-mail.* 3d ed. Hauppauge, N.Y.: Barron's Educational Series, 2004.

Clark, Roy Peter. *Writing Tools: 50 Essential Strategies for Every Writer.* New York: Little, Brown and Company, 2008.

Griffin, Jack. *How to Say It at Work: Power Words, Phrases, and Communication Secrets for Getting Ahead.* 2d ed. Upper Saddle River, N.J.: Prentice Hall Press, 2008.

Oliu, Walter E., Charles T. Brusaw, and Gerald J. Alred. *Writing That Works: Communicating Effectively on the Job.* 9th ed. Boston: Bedford/St. Martin's, 2006.

Plotnik, Arthur. *Spunk & Bite: A Writer's Guide to Bold, Contemporary Style.* Random House Reference, 2007.

VanHuss, Susan H. *Basic Letter and Memo Writing.* 5th ed. Florence, Ky.: South-Western Educational Publishing, 2004.

not coincidentally, is the purpose for the call. And the conclusion, "thanks for calling" or "goodbye," brings an end to the communication.

Written communication also has a beginning, middle, and end. Memos are no exception.

The beginning of any piece of writing has one aim—to get the reader to read further. If the first chapter of a novel is dull, the reader will close the book. If the first paragraph of a newspaper story (called the "lead") doesn't capture the reader's attention, the reader will likely turn the page to find a story that does.

People do not read every piece of writing they're handed. If they did, those guys passing out pamphlets on street corners would have it a lot easier.

If your boss requests a memo on a certain topic or event, you will have a reader whether you want one or not. One good rule of thumb is this: If the reader (your boss, for instance) is expecting the memo, begin the memo with a summary of its content. If the reader is not expecting the memo, begin with something that will ensure the person will read the memo.

Regardless of the communication medium you use, you need to structure and manage the contents of your presentation into a beginning, a middle, and an end.

DID YOU KNOW?

Employers surveyed in 2007 by the National Association of Colleges and Employers rated communication skills (verbal and written) as very-to-extremely important for job candidates.

TIPS ON MEMO WRITING

According to Emily Thrush, author of an essay titled *How to Write a Memo*, several steps should be followed when writing a professional memo.

The heading information should include the following information:

- the date
- the names of the writer and reader of the memo
- the subject of the memo (also referred to as the statement of purpose)

Other tips for successful memo writing are as follows:

- Avoid writing long paragraphs of dense text.

- Use bulleted lists as well as bolded or underlined text to draw attention to important points.

- Use strong, active verbs and avoid the passive voice. For example, instead of saying "By June 1 the report will be completed by marketing," say, "Marketing will complete the report by June 1." Note the more decisive tone in the second example, as compared to the use of the passive voice in the first.

- The ending of the memo may differ from office to office. Generally, the standard "Please contact me if you have any questions" is considered appropriate, but some professionals prefer a more formal closing.

Most memos:

- Communicate the data in narrative form

- Are accompanied by a table or graph if the narrative text includes a lot of numerical data. (Tables and graphs are discussed in detail in Chapter 6.)

- Have subheads for each section and subsection

- Have subheads that are informative

✔ TRUE OR FALSE: ANSWERS

Do You Know How to Effectively Communicate Information?

1. It's important to fit every last bit of information into a 10-minute presentation.

False. Your presentation should be clear and concise, not a recitation of every fact or finding you discovered during your research. However, you might have the opportunity to use this additional information in a question-and-answer session after your presentation or in a later meeting.

2. A good presentation has two main components: the body and the conclusion.

False. A good presentation actually has three main components: the introduction, body, and the conclusion. You should never just launch into the body of your speech. A good presentation begins by grabbing the audience's attention, detailing the basic topic of your speech and connecting it to the audience, and previewing the main points of the presentation. Once you do this, you can move on to the body of the presentation.

3. Memos should contain long, dense paragraphs to provide as much information to the reader as possible.

False. Well-written memos are concise and visually attractive. They feature short declarative sentences; strong, active verbs; descriptive subheads; and bulleted lists and bolded or underlined text (when appropriate).

IN SUMMARY . . .

- Presentations should have an introduction, a body, and a conclusion.

- While delivering an oral presentation, speak loudly and clearly, maintain eye contact with the audience, and be prepared to answer questions related to the topic.

- Don't try to cram too much into one presentation or memo—this will only confuse the reader or audience and cause them to lose interest.

- Specify three or four main points in a presentation and describe them once you've caught the audience's attention with an interesting introduction.

- When writing a memo, begin with a summary of the content. A professional memo is concise and easy to follow.

- Vary the appearance of a memo by using bullets or bolded text to catch the reader's attention.

MAKING THE
PRESENTATION
FIT THE DATA

As Chapter 5 illustrates, you can be on your way to giving an effective presentation by acquiring information, remaining focused, and being organized, whether you are responsible for a written memo or an oral report.

However, you can be the most organized, focused, and prepared presenter, but your presentation can still fail. A good presentation consists of not only what you communicate, but the tools you use. Some information can best be presented in a narrative form. Other kinds of information, such as quantitative data, are best presented in graphic form.

INFOGRAPHICS

You've probably heard the old adage, "Seeing is believing." You're also intelligent enough to know

✔ TRUE OR FALSE?

Do You Know How to Use Infographics?

1. Quantitative data is best presented in narrative form.

2. Line graphs are most effective at demonstrating that something is larger than something else.

3. Infographics should be easy to read and get straight to the point.

4. When creating infographics, it's extremely important to know what style (bar graph, line graph, pie chart, etc.) will work best for your audience.

Test yourself as you read through this chapter. The answers appear on pages 123–124.

that you cannot always believe everything you see, read, hear, think, or feel. But there are still times—and a presentation is one of them—when visual aids can help you organize your information in such a way that people can grasp it. The following sections describe the most common infographics, which are also referred to as informational graphics.

Bar Graphs

The bar graph is perhaps the most commonly used chart. Its real value is in demonstrating that some-

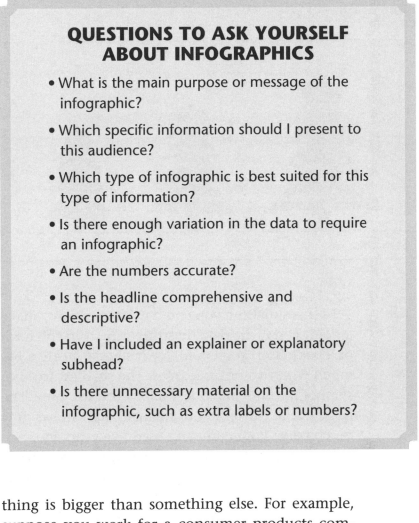

QUESTIONS TO ASK YOURSELF ABOUT INFOGRAPHICS

- What is the main purpose or message of the infographic?

- Which specific information should I present to this audience?

- Which type of infographic is best suited for this type of information?

- Is there enough variation in the data to require an infographic?

- Are the numbers accurate?

- Is the headline comprehensive and descriptive?

- Have I included an explainer or explanatory subhead?

- Is there unnecessary material on the infographic, such as extra labels or numbers?

thing is bigger than something else. For example, suppose you work for a consumer products company that makes bath soap. You have been assigned the task of speaking to the local chapter of the Sierra Club about how much less paper your company uses now compared to five years ago.

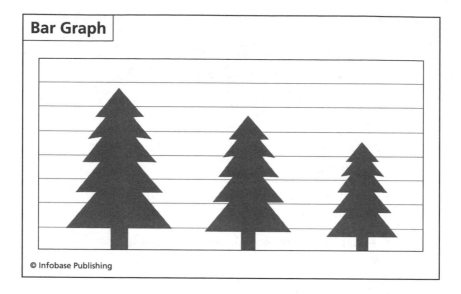

Bar Graph

© Infobase Publishing

In this situation, you could most effectively make a point about the data by structuring it in the form of a bar graph. You could, for instance, create a bar graph with two or three trees. The smallest tree is a symbol for how much less paper you use now. The huge tree at the far left of the bar graph shows how much paper your company used five years ago.

Be aware that a bar graph with more than three bars can become cumbersome and complicate your goal.

Line Graphs

Just as bar graphs are most effective at showing comparisons, line graphs are most effective at showing change over time. For instance, they can be used to show salary trends of employees who know how to give effective presentations versus those who do not. Line graphs work best when you have many observations over a period of time.

Pie Charts

Pie charts are used almost exclusively to show the totality of something sliced up into parts. For example, if you wanted to show which sports the members of your debate team prefer to watch on television, a pie chart would be an effective tool.

By slicing up the pie, you could show that 35 percent prefer football; 25 percent basketball; 20 percent baseball; and 20 percent other sports.

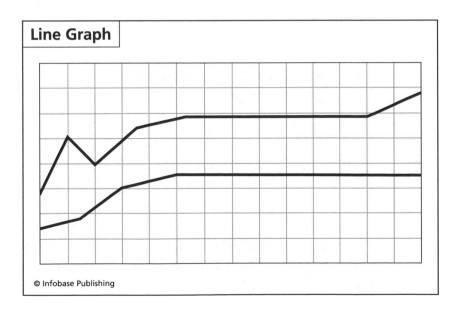

Line Graph

© Infobase Publishing

During a meeting, workers study a variety of infographics, including bar graphs, line graphs, and pie charts. (Tom & Dee Ann McCarthy, Corbis)

CREATING AND PRESENTING INFOGRAPHICS

The function of an infographic is to convey information in a visual form. It should be easy to read and should get straight to the point. A complicated, jumbled, or confusing graph is pointless. In other words, an infographic should present information to an audience or reader in a way that is visually appealing and quickly understood. Just like memos and oral presentations, infographics have a beginning, a middle, and an end.

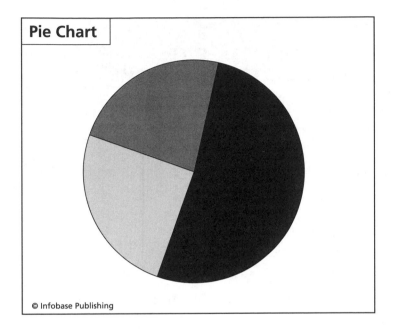

Pie Chart

© Infobase Publishing

Beginning

- Make sure your graphic has an easy-to-read headline. It should be as short and catchy as possible.

- Make sure your graphic has an *explainer* beneath the headline. An explainer is a subhead consisting of a few words explaining the graphic and why the information presented is important. (Caution: The explainer should add to the information in the graphic rather than simply restate it.)

SURF THE WEB: PIE CHARTS AND GRAPHS

Create a Graph
http://nces.ed.gov/nceskids/createagraph/default.aspx

GraphCharts.com
http://www.graphscharts.com

Graphing Resources
http://www.ncsu.edu/labwrite/res/gh/gh-bargraph.html

Microsoft Office Online: Excel: Present Your Data in a Pie Chart
http://office.microsoft.com/en-us/excel/HA102118481033.aspx

Pie Charts
http://www.statcan.gc.ca/edu/power-pouvoir/ch9/pie-secteurs/5214826-eng.htm

Using Data and Statistics
http://www.mathleague.com/help/data/data.htm

Middle

The body of the infographic is the data presented graphically. Besides the line graphs, bar graphs, and pie charts we have covered, the data in an info-

BOOKS TO READ: INFOGRAPHICS

Bluttman, Ken. *Excel Charts For Dummies*. Hoboken, N.J.: For Dummies, 2005.

Cohen, Sandee. *Macromedia FreeHand MX for Windows & Macintosh*. Berkeley, Calif.: Peachpit Press, 2003.

Few, Stephen. *Show Me the Numbers: Designing Tables and Graphs to Enlighten*. Oakland, Calif.: Analytics Press, 2004.

George-Palilonis, Jennifer. *A Practical Guide to Graphics Reporting: Information Graphics for Print, Web & Broadcast*. Burlington, Mass.: Focal Press, 2006.

Golding, Mordy. *Real World Adobe Illustrator CS3*. 2d ed. Berkeley, Calif.: Peachpit Press, 2007.

Jacobs, Kathy, Curt Frye, and Doug Frye. *Excel 2007 Charts Made Easy Series*. San Francisco: McGraw-Hill Osborne Media, 2008.

Robbins, Naomi B. *Creating More Effective Graphs*. Hoboken, N.J.: Wiley-Interscience, 2004.

Tufte, Edward R. *The Visual Display of Quantitative Information*. 2d ed. Cheshire, Conn.: Graphics Press, 2001.

Zelazny, Gene. *The Say It with Charts Complete Toolkit*. New York: McGraw-Hill, 2006.

Line graphs are most effective at showing change over time. (Jack Dempsey, Associated Press)

graphic can be a map or drawing. *USA Today* has set the standard in the newspaper business for its use of infographics.

End

The infographic should have a source listed at the bottom, which informs the reader where the information comes from. In the debate-team pie chart example, the source would merely be something like "based on a recent series of interviews by John Smith."

Infographics can sometimes be hand-drawn, but are much more commonly created on computer. Computer-generated infographics look much more professional and are most often expected in a business

SURF THE WEB: INFOGRAPHICS

American Institute of Graphic Arts
  http://www.aiga.org

Dynamic Graphics
  http://www.dynamicgraphics.com

HOW
  http://www.howdesign.com

Information Design Journal
  http://www.benjamins.com/cgi-bin/
    t_seriesview.cgi?series=IDJ

Society for News Design
  http://www.snd.org

setting. Several computer-software programs, such as Adobe Freehand and Adobe Illustrator, are designed specifically to help you create infographics.

USA Today *has come out with a new survey— apparently, three out of four people make up 75 percent of the population.*

—**David Letterman, comedian and late-night talk show host**

CONSIDER THE AUDIENCE

In addition to considering which tools will best present your information, you need to take your audience into account when you select the tools for your presentation. Marcus learned that the hard way.

Near the end of his first year with a publishing firm, Marcus, an accountant, was asked to make a presentation on cost cutting to the company. Because it was a reasonably large company, Marcus decided it would be more effective to give several smaller presentations to individual departments than trying to speak to the whole company at one time. His boss agreed.

"The first thing I did was decide on an oral presentation instead of a memo," Marcus said. "A lengthy memo on cost cutting would be counterproductive. I also figured that if I approached each department one-on-one, I could answer questions and my colleagues would be able to put a face on this financial stuff."

Knowing that an effective presentation would reflect well on him, Marcus planned meticulously. He gathered the figures he would need. He arranged for the use of overheads for pie charts and bar graphs. He even rehearsed his presentation in front of his girlfriend.

"The first presentation went real well," Marcus said. "The marketing staff seemed to get the message. I got a few laughs. I could answer all their questions. I thought the whole thing was in the bag."

On the very next day, the very same presentation was a disaster.

"I was blown away," Marcus said. "Nothing worked. I couldn't believe it."

The presentation had been given to the editorial department. All of Marcus's fancy bar graphs, figures, and tables went over like a lead balloon with people who dealt in the currency of words, whereas the marketing personnel, who were more comfortable with numbers, appreciated the infographics. Marcus understood his purpose and goals. He knew his stuff. He rehearsed. What he didn't do was take the time to consider his audience.

"It's the kind of mistake you only have to make once," Marcus said. "I'm glad I made it early in my career."

To avoid making the same mistake Marcus did, make sure that you find out who your audience will be ahead of time. Do some research on this audience so you know which methods will target them most effectively.

✔ TRUE OR FALSE: ANSWERS

Do You Know How to Use Infographics?

1. Quantitative data is best presented in narrative form.

False. Quantitative data gets lost amid mountains of words and paragraphs if it's presented in narrative form. It is best presented in graphic form by using graphs and charts known as infographics.

2. Line graphs are most effective at demonstrating that something is larger than something else.

False. Line graphs are most effective when you want to show change over time. Use bar graphs to demonstrate differences in size.

3. Infographics should be easy to read and get straight to the point.

True. Including unnecessary text and too many graphics can be confusing to the reader.

4. When creating infographics, it's extremely important to know what style (bar graph, line graph, pie chart, etc.) will work best for your audience.

True. Everyone processes information differently, so it is important that you conduct research to determine which infographic will be most effective for your target group.

IN SUMMARY . . .

- Informational graphics, or infographics, are good for presenting data visually during a presentation.

- Bar graphs demonstrate that something is larger than something else.

- Line graphs are best at showing change over time.

- Pie charts should be used to illustrate the totality of something sliced into parts.

- All infographics should have a beginning, a middle, and an end. They should be visually interesting and easy to understand.

- Before preparing materials for a presentation, it is important to know your audience and decide which types of infographics will most effectively target them.

STAYING SANE IN THE INFORMATION AGE

The more you know, the more you need to know. Especially when it comes to the Internet or nearly anything else related to technology, things are changing too quickly to keep up. Even though more than 220 million Americans were using the Internet when this book was written, by the time you read this, that number will have already grown. So just because you know a fact now does not mean it will be always and forever correct.

Recently there has been talk that Egypt—not Greece—was the real hotbed of intellectual activity in the ancient world. In addition, Pluto is no longer the ninth planet in our solar system. It has been downgraded to the status of "dwarf planet," because "it has not become gravitationally dominant and it shares its orbital space with other bodies of a similar size," according to *National Geographic*. (Just when

✔ TRUE OR FALSE?

Do You Know How to Avoid Information Overload?

1. Some information is more stable than others.

2. It's important to set a clear goal before you begin to conduct research.

3. It's important to continue to learn and keep an open mind about new information resources.

Test yourself as you read through this chapter. The answers appear on pages 134–135.

you were sure there were nine planets, huh?) As you can see, information is always subject to change.

☛ FACT

A recent survey detailed in the *New York Times* found that 72 percent of Americans were recent Internet users, up from 59 percent in 2000.

STABILITY OF INFORMATION

As you learned earlier in the book (Chapter 3), evaluating information is a critical part of doing research and making presentations. The source from which you receive the information can have a lot to do with how reliable that information is.

Although all information is subject to change, some facts are less likely to change. Much of the time, you can use your common sense to figure out the stability of basic pieces of information. For example, which of the following pieces of information are not likely to change in your lifetime?

1. The sun's distance from Earth
2. The number of Web pages
3. The number of countries in the world
4. The number of languages spoken in the world
5. The best way to treat the common cold
6. The nature of a college education
7. The fact that your mother and father give you advice on nearly every aspect of your life
8. The number of bones in a human body
9. The current world record for running a mile
10. The number of U.S. presidents who served in office in the 19th century

If you answered 1, 8, and 10, you are correct. You can easily prove these facts with a large amount of scientific and historical evidence. For example, you can easily look up the number of U.S. presidents who were in office during the 19th century—that number (24) cannot change and is recorded in many sources.

Racing records are examples of information that will most likely change over time. (Bob Daemmrich, The Image Works)

However, in all the other examples, what's true in one time or context may not always be true in another, as Jason found out to his embarrassment.

Jason worked his way through high school and college as a construction laborer. He had dug many footers in his years as a laborer. Having lived in the South his whole life, Jason knew that a footer should be between 12 and 18 inches deep, so that frost cannot get under it and heave the brick after it settles. He knew his stuff and felt confident as a laborer.

On a vacation to upstate New York, Jason and his family went out for lunch. The restaurant was crowded, and they were told they'd have a 30-minute wait until they could be seated.

While he waited, Jason noticed a construction crew building a house next door to the restaurant.

"I walked over to the guys, you know, wanting to talk one construction worker to another," Jason said. "Two minutes later, I felt like an idiot."

Jason struck up a conversation with a laborer who happened to be digging a footer for the house's front porch. He told the northern laborer that he was digging deeper than he had to.

"I told him he was already deep enough," Jason said. "The guy just looked at me like I was trying to be a smart guy. Actually, I was being anything but smart. I should have asked a couple of questions instead of trying to strut my stuff."

What Jason did not know was that just because something is true at point A does not mean it is true at point B. You see, in the South, footers can be shallower because it does not generally get as cold as it does up North. In the North, the frost line is at least 36 inches.

"Even though I never worked in construction again after I graduated from college," Jason said, "I learned a valuable lesson from that laborer: Never assume that the same rules apply everywhere—there may be more to it than you think."

Just because something is true at point A does not mean it is true at point B.

GROWTH IN NUMBER OF WEB SITES

September 1993	204
August 1996	342,081
August 2000	19,823,296
August 2005	70,392,567
November 2006	101,435,253

Source: Hobbes Internet Timeline

When men are most sure and arrogant they are commonly most mistaken, giving views to passion without that proper deliberation which alone can secure them from the grossest absurdities.

—David Hume, Scottish philosopher and historian

HOW DO I KEEP UP WITH INFORMATION WITHOUT GOING CRAZY?

As you know by now, information overload can be overwhelming. Just think back when you, your siblings, and a couple of your friends all shouted different times, schedules, and needs at your mother at the same time. Chances are she shut down, you became quiet, and she asked for the information again. Only this time, she demanded to be allowed to focus on one thing at a time.

The same will be true for you. As we have seen in the personal examples, each of the young people had to establish a clear goal before they could successfully seek and find the information they actually needed. Andy had to learn about the shopping habits of mothers and babies; Brendan had to learn more about the wolves of the Rockies; Deleasa had to suddenly manage a new set of information.

By the time you get out of school and have worked part-time jobs, participated in extracurricular activities, and practiced the research and information-management skills discussed in this book, you should have a foundation on which to build. After that, it will be a matter of keeping up with what's new in your field.

Minds are like parachutes. They only function when they are open.

—Lord Thomas Dewar, English author

For instance, companies around the world are doing all they can to improve their productivity through the use of technology and computers. If you were in the workforce right now, computers would

Whatever the situation, you will always be acquiring, evaluating, maintaining, organizing, and presenting information.

likely play a major role in how you do your job, just as a computer is a more essential part of schoolwork now than it was 10 years ago. Whatever the situation, you will always be acquiring, evaluating, maintaining, organizing, and presenting information.

KNOW WHAT YOU CAN

Remember this: You will never know all there is to know. Doing so is impossible. Staying current in your field and keeping your mind open to learning more about the world you live in will be your best way to keep from going crazy in the Information Age.

✔ TRUE OR FALSE: ANSWERS

Do You Know How to Avoid Information Overload?

1. Some information is more stable than others.

True. George Washington will always be the first president of the United States, but other information may not stay the same. For example, the names of countries in Africa, the number of planets in our solar system, the location of Boeing's headquarters, and the number of wolves in Yellowstone National Park may change over time. When conducting research, it's important to know the difference between information that is concrete in nature and information that may change over time.

2. It's important to set a clear goal before you begin to conduct research.

True. Otherwise you'll get distracted by the wealth of information that is available about a particular subject.

3. It's important to continue to learn and keep an open mind about new information resources.

True. The world of information never stops changing and growing. To be successful in the workplace, you need to always seek out the most current information, as well as new methods to gather, analyze, and present it.

IN SUMMARY . . .

- Remember that what is true in one context is not necessarily true in another.
- Set a clear goal before you start your search for information.
- Keep an open mind and pay attention to changes in your field to keep from going crazy in the Information Age.
- Technology is changing very rapidly, and it is impossible to ever know all there is to know.

WEB SITES

Copyright

United States Copyright Office
http://www.copyright.gov

Evaluating Information

Evaluating Information Sources: Basic Principles
http://library.duke.edu/services/instruction/
libraryguide/evaluating.html

Evaluating Internet Sources and Sites: A Tutorial
http://www.lib.purdue.edu/ugrl/staff/sharkey/
interneteval

Evaluating Web Pages
http://library.duke.edu/services/instruction/
libraryguide/evalwebpages.html

Evaluating Web Sites: Criteria and Tools
http://www.library.cornell.edu/olinuris/ref/
research/webeval.html

Five Criteria for Evaluating Web Pages
http://www.nmc.edu/library/how/internet/five.
html

The Good, the Bad, and the Ugly or, Why It's a
Good Idea to Evaluate Web Sources
http://lib.nmsu.edu/instruction/evalcrit.html

How Do I Evaluate Internet Resources?
http://www.bc.edu/libraries/help/howdoi/
howto/evaluateinternet.html

General

How Stuff Works: How Web Pages Work
http://www.howstuffworks.com/web-page.htm

MindTools.com: Information and Study Skills
http://www.mindtools.com/pages/main/
newMN_ISS.htm

The Research Process: A Step-by-Step Guide
http://valenciacc.edu/library/west/research/sbs_
primarySecondary.asp

Infographics

American Institute of Graphic Arts
http://www.aiga.org

Create a Graph
http://nces.ed.gov/nceskids/createagraph/
default.aspx

Dynamic Graphics
http://www.dynamicgraphics.com

GraphCharts.com
  http://www.graphscharts.com

Graphing Resources
  http://www.ncsu.edu/labwrite/res/gh/
  gh-bargraph.html

HOW
  http://www.howdesign.com

Information Design Journal
  http://www.benjamins.com/cgi-bin/t_seriesview.
  cgi?series=IDJ

Microsoft Office Online: Excel: Present Your Data
  in a Pie Chart
  http://office.microsoft.com/en-us/excel/
  HA102118481033.aspx

Pie Charts
  http://www.statcan.gc.ca/edu/power-pouvoir/
  ch9/pie-secteurs/5214826-eng.htm

Society for News Design
  http://www.snd.org

Using Data and Statistics
  http://www.mathleague.com/help/data/data.htm

Organization

National Association of Professional Organizers:
  Office Organizing Tips
  http://www.napo.net/public/Org_tips/office_tips.
  asp

Plagiarism

Avoiding Plagiarism
  http://owl.english.purdue.edu/owl/
  resource/589/01

Center for Academic Integrity
  http://www.academicintegrity.org

Plagiarism Lessons
  http://www.mtlsd.org/highschool/
  highschoolplagiarismlessons.asp

PlagiarismToday
  http://www.plagiarismtoday.com

Plagiarism: What It is and How to Recognize and
  Avoid It
  http://www.indiana.edu/~wts/pamphlets/
  plagiarism.shtml

Students' Guide to Preventing and Avoiding
  Plagiarism
  http://www.liunet.edu/cwis/cwp/library/
  exhibits/plagstudent.htm

Presentations/Public Speaking

Effective Presentations
  http://www.research.ucla.edu/era/present

How to Deliver Effective Presentations
  http://www.ehow.com/how_2265462_deliver-
  effective-presentations.html?ref=fuel&utm_
  source=yahoo&utm_medium=ssp&utm_
  campaign=yssp_art

Humor in Public Speaking
http://www.msstate.edu/org/toastmasters/
resources/humor_in_speaking.pdf

Making Effective Oral Presentations
http://web.cba.neu.edu/~ewertheim/skills/oral.
htm

Presentations.com
http://www.presentations.com

Top 10 Tips for Creating Successful Business
Presentations
http://presentationsoft.about.com/od/
powerpointinbusiness/tp/bus_pres_tips.htm

WannaLearn.com: Personal Enrichment: Public
Speaking
http://www.wannalearn.com/
Personal_Enrichment/Public_Speaking

Primary and Secondary Sources

Library Research Using Primary Sources
http://www.aurora.edu/library/primarysources.
htm

Primary Resources
http://www.lib.berkeley.edu/instruct/guides/
primarysources.html

Primary vs. Secondary Sources
http://valenciacc.edu/library/west/research/sbs_
primarySecondary.asp

The Research Process: A Step-by-Step Guide
http://valenciacc.edu/library/west/research/sbs_
primarySecondary.asp

Using Primary Sources on the Web
http://www.ala.org/ala/mgrps/divs/rusa/
resources/usingprimarysources/index.cfm

Using Sources Effectively in Your Own Writing
http://www.mals.duke.edu/Using_Sources.pdf

Spreadsheets

About.com: Spreadsheets
http://spreadsheets.about.com/od/?once=true&

Answers.com: Spreadsheet
http://www.answers.com/topic/spreadsheet

The Spreadsheet Page for Excel Users and
Developers
http://spreadsheetpage.com

Web Browsers

AOL Explorer
http://downloads.channel.aol.com/browser

Avant Browser
http://www.avantbrowser.com

Flock
http://www.flock.com

Google Chrome
http://www.google.com/chrome

Internet Explorer
http://www.microsoft.com/windows/downloads/
ie/getitnow.mspx

K-Meleon
http://kmeleon.sourceforge.net

Konqueror
http://www.konqueror.org

Mozilla Firefox
http://www.mozilla.com/en-US/firefox

Opera
http://www.opera.com

Safari
http://www.apple.com/safari

Writing

About.com: Writing Skills
http://careerplanning.about.com/cs/miscskills/a/
writing_skills.htm

GLOSSARY

body the middle section of a presentation or memo, which contains the key points and includes the majority of the total information

copyright a form of legal protection of original works of authorship including literary, musical, dramatic, and artistic works

database a collection of information that is organized in a systematic way

empiricism a 17th-century British theory stating that all knowledge is derived from sensory experience, by observation and experimentation

euphemism vague, inoffensive words used to hide or dress up facts

explainer a subhead on an infographic that explains the graphic's purpose; should add to the title, rather than simply restate it

field in a database, a specific category of information; for example, contact information is divided into fields, such as address, telephone number, and email address

infographic a representation of data in the form of a graph, chart, or map that is used as a visual aid in a presentation; also referred to as informational graphics

information presentation a presentation whose primary goal is to convey information on an area of expertise, such as technology, methods, procedures, or policies

Internet the name for the vast collection of interconnected computer networks around the world

mail merge in a word-processing program, a short cut that enables two or more document files to be combined into one file

"paperless office" a work environment where all information is stored on computers, rather than in paper documents

plagiarism using (quoting or paraphrasing) somebody else's words and claiming or pretending they're your own words

primary sources any firsthand information such as a letter written by a former president or an eyewitness account

record in a database, an organized compilation of related fields

search engine computer software used to locate specific information

secondary sources reports or analyses of information drawn from other sources

spreadsheet a large grid composed of rows and columns that enables you to organize data and lay out information about transactions; it "spreads" or shows all of the costs, income, taxes, etc. in an organized way for a manager to refer to when making a decision

Web browser a computer program used to facilitate access to Web sites or information on a network

World Wide Web interconnected information residing on the Internet

word-processing program a computer program that helps people edit and type documents quicker and more precisely

BIBLIOGRAPHY

Anderson, Chalon E., Amy T. Carrell, and Jimmyl Widdifield. *What Every Student Should Know About Citing Sources with APA Documentation.* Boston: Allyn & Bacon, 2006.

Aslett, Don. *The Office Clutter Cure.* 2d ed. Cincinnati, Ohio: Marsh Creek Press, 2008.

Baig, Edward C. *Macs For Dummies.* 10th ed. Hoboken, N.J.: For Dummies, 2008.

Bell, Arthur H. *Butterflies Be Gone: An 8-Step Approach to Sweat-Proof Public Speaking.* New York: McGraw-Hill, 2008.

———. *Writing Effective Letters, Memos, and E-mail.* 3d ed. Hauppauge, N.Y.: Barron's Educational Series, 2004.

Benjamin, Susan J. *Speak with Success: A Student's Step-by-Step Guide to Fearless Public Speaking.* Tucson, Ariz.: Good Year Books, 2007.

Bluttman, Ken. *Excel Charts For Dummies.* Hoboken, N.J.: For Dummies, 2005.

Browne, M. Neil, and Stuart M. Keeley. *Asking the Right Questions: A Guide to Critical Thinking.* 8th ed. Upper Saddle River, N.J.: Prentice Hall, 2006.

Clark, Roy Peter. *Writing Tools: 50 Essential Strategies for Every Writer.* New York: Little, Brown and Company, 2008.

Cohen, Sandee. *Macromedia FreeHand MX for Windows & Macintosh.* Berkeley, Calif.: Peachpit Press, 2003.

Creswell, John W. *Research Design: Qualitative, Quantitative, and Mixed Methods Approaches.* 3d ed. Thousand Oaks, Calif.: Sage Publications, 2008.

Davenport, Liz. *Order from Chaos: A Six-Step Plan for Organizing Yourself, Your Office, and Your Life.* New York: Three Rivers Press, 2001.

Denzin, Norman K., and Yvonna Lincoln. *The SAGE Handbook of Qualitative Research.* 3d ed. Thousand Oaks, Calif.: Sage Publications, 2005.

Few, Stephen. *Show Me the Numbers: Designing Tables and Graphs to Enlighten.* Oakland, Calif.: Analytics Press, 2004.

George-Palilonis, Jennifer. *A Practical Guide to Graphics Reporting: Information Graphics for Print, Web & Broadcast.* Burlington, Mass.: Focal Press, 2006.

Golding, Mordy. *Real World Adobe Illustrator CS3.* 2d ed. Berkeley, Calif.: Peachpit Press, 2007.

Gookin, Dan. *PCs For Dummies*. 11th ed. Hoboken, N.J.: For Dummies, 2007.

Griffin, Jack. *How to Say It at Work: Power Words, Phrases, and Communication Secrets for Getting Ahead*. 2d ed. Upper Saddle River, N.J.: Prentice Hall Press, 2008.

Hansen, Dhawn, and Tracey Turner. *Organize Your Office and Manage Your Time: A Be Smart Girls Guide*. Bloomington, Ind.: iUniverse Inc., 2007.

Jacobs, Kathy, Curt Frye, and Doug Frye. *Excel 2007 Charts Made Easy Series*. San Francisco: McGraw-Hill Osborne Media, 2008.

Kendall-Tackett, Kathleen. *The Well-Ordered Office: How to Create an Efficient and Serene Workspace*. Oakland, Calif.: New Harbinger Publications, 2005.

Klaus, Peggy. *The Hard Truth About Soft Skills: Workplace Lessons Smart People Wish They'd Learned Sooner*. New York: Collins Business, 2008.

Kushner, Malcolm. *Public Speaking For Dummies*. 2d ed. Hoboken, N.J.: For Dummies, 2004.

Levine, John R., Margaret Levine Young, and Carol Baroudi. *The Internet For Dummies*. 11th ed. Hoboken, N.J.: For Dummies, 2007.

Lipson, Charles. *Doing Honest Work in College: How to Prepare Citations, Avoid Plagiarism, and Achieve Real Academic Success*. Chicago: University of Chicago Press, 2004.

Macinnis, J. Lyman. *The Elements of Great Public Speaking: How to Be Calm, Confident, and Compelling.* Berkeley, Calif.: Ten Speed Press, 2006.

Maxey, Cyndi, and Kevin E. O'Connor. *Speak Up!: A Woman's Guide to Presenting Like a Pro.* New York: St. Martin's Griffin, 2008.

Nakone, Lanna, and Arlene Taylor. *Organizing for Your Brain Type: Finding Your Own Solution to Managing Time, Paper, and Stuff.* New York: St. Martin's Griffin, 2005.

Nelson, Mike. *Clutter Proof Your Business: Turn Your Mess into Success.* Franklin Lakes, N.J.: Career Press, 2002.

Oliu, Walter E., Charles T. Brusaw, and Gerald J. Alred. *Writing That Works: Communicating Effectively on the Job.* 9th ed. Boston: Bedford/St. Martin's, 2006.

Oppel, Andrew. *Databases Demystified.* San Francisco: McGraw-Hill Osborne Media, 2004.

Plotnik, Arthur. *Spunk & Bite: A Writer's Guide to Bold, Contemporary Style.* Random House Reference, 2007.

Posner, Richard A. *The Little Book of Plagiarism.* New York: Pantheon Books, 2007.

Robbins, Naomi B. *Creating More Effective Graphs.* Hoboken, N.J.: Wiley-Interscience, 2004.

Rockmore, Alicia, and Sarah Welch. *Everything (almost) In Its Place: Control Chaos, Conquer Clutter, and Get Organized the Buttoned Up Way.* New York: St. Martin's Griffin, 2008.

Silber, Lee. *Organizing from the Right Side of the Brain: A Creative Approach to Getting Organized.* New York: St. Martin's Griffin, 2004.

Stern, Linda. *What Every Student Should Know About Avoiding Plagiarism.* New York: Longman Publishing Group, 2006.

Tufte, Edward R. *The Visual Display of Quantitative Information.* 2d ed. Cheshire, Conn.: Graphics Press, 2001.

VanHuss, Susan H. *Basic Letter and Memo Writing.* 5th ed. Florence, Ky.: South-Western Educational Publishing, 2004.

Weissman, Jerry. *Presenting to Win: The Art of Telling Your Story.* Upper Saddle River, N.J.: Prentice Hall, 2006.

Zelazny, Gene. *Say It with Presentations.* Rev. ed. 2d ed. New York: McGraw-Hill, 2006.

———. *The Say It with Charts Complete Toolkit.* New York: McGraw-Hill, 2006.

Zeoli, Richard. *The 7 Principles of Public Speaking: Proven Methods from a PR Professional.* New York: Skyhorse Publishing, 2008.

Index